Anonymous

The Home Rule Bill in Committee, Session 1893

Anonymous

The Home Rule Bill in Committee, Session 1893

ISBN/EAN: 9783337160180

Printed in Europe, USA, Canada, Australia, Japan

Cover: Foto ©ninafisch / pixelio.de

More available books at **www.hansebooks.com**

THE HOME RULE BILL

IN COMMITTEE,

SESSION 1893,

WITH INDEX.

PRICE SIXPENCE.

SECOND EDITION.

PRINTED AND PUBLISHED BY THE IRISH UNIONIST ALLIANCE
DUBLIN: 109 GRAFTON STREET.
LONDON: 26, PALACE CHAMBERS, BRIDGE STREET, WESTMINSTER

The following pages present, in the briefest possible form, the History of the Home Rule Bill of 1893 in Committee. The publication has been compiled with the object of supplying a ready reference to the discussion on the Bill during its progress through that stage.

The Clauses are printed exactly as in the Bill.

The letters " P.D." and " T.D." refer to the publications known as the " Parliamentary Debates " and " Times Debates " respectively.

The Clauses (those discussed) are also set out as amended, additions being printed in italics, and the portions struck out printed within brackets.

An exhaustive Index appears at the close, and appended the reader will find an analysis of the principal divisions, showing the British Majorities against the proposals of the Government.

THE BILL IN COMMITTEE.

Clause 1.

PART I.

Legislative Authority.

1. *On and after the appointed day* there shall be in Ireland a Legislature consisting of Her Majesty the Queen and of two Houses, the Legislative Council and the Legislative Assembly.

The debates on this Clause extended over five sittings, and lasted 29 hours. (May 8, 9, 10, 11, 12.)

Prior to the amendment being discussed—

Mr. CHAMBERLAIN moved the postponement of all clauses up to Clause IX.—(P.D., vol. XII., p. 347; T.D., vol. XXIV., p. 6.)

In the course of the debate—

Mr. GLADSTONE, referring to Clause 9, said the Government "intended to propose the plan embodied in the Bill."—(P.D., vol. XII., p. 356; T.D., vol. XXIV., p. 8.)

Mr. Arthur Balfour, Mr. Timothy Healy, and Mr. James Lowther took part in the debate.

The Committee divided—

For Postponement	213
Against	270
Majority ...	57

(Division List No. 67.)

On **Mr. DARLING'S** Amendment—page 1, line 11—before "on," insert:—

> "*Without in any way impairing, restricting or altering the supreme power and authority of Parliament in all matters, as well Local as Imperial, and over all persons in Great Britain and Ireland.*"

Mr. DARLING quoted Mr. Parnell on Ireland's claim to nationhood.--(P.D., vol. XII., p. 362; T.D., vol. XXIV., p. 10.)

The Government's objections were based on two grounds:—

(1) The sufficiency of the Preamble;

(2) The undesirability of limiting the supremacy by clause.

The Debate was remarkable for Mr. Gladstone's apologies for the "inconsiderate and dangerous claims" previously put forward by Parnellites; and the Right Hon. gentleman's claim that Mr. Parnell had fully accepted the Bill of 1886.—(P.D., vol. XII., p. 368; T.D., vol. XXIV., p. 11.)

After four hours' discussion and closure resolution,

The Committee divided—

For the Amendment	233
Against the Amendment	285
Majority ...	52

(Division List No. 69.)

Mr. BARTLEY moved:—

page 1, line 11, after word "Ireland" to insert:—

"*subordinate to Parliament.*"

(P.D., vol. XII., p. 465; T.D., vol. XXIV., p. 28.)

Mr. GLADSTONE refused on grounds :—
  (1) Amendment would weaken supremacy;
  (2) It would be a bar sinister on Irish legislature.
    (P.D. vol. XII., p. 469; T.D., vol. XXIV., p. 29.)

Mr. HOBHOUSE quoted Mr. John Redmond on the "formal compact."—(P.D., vol. XII., p. 473; T.D., vol. XXIV. p. 30.)

LORD CRANBORNE quoted Home Secretary's promise that such a clause would be accepted.—(P.D., vol. XII., p. 475; T.D., vol. XXIV., p. 30.)

Mr. BLAKE quoted Mr. Parnell and Mr. Chamberlain in 1886.—(P.D., vol. XII., p. 479, 81; T.D.. vol. XXIV., p. 31.)

Lord Randolph Churchill, Mr. Goschen, Mr. Haldane, Col. Saunderson and others spoke.

After two hours' discussion

The Committee divided—

For the Amendment	257
Against the Amendment	292
Majority	35

(Division List No. 74.)

Mr. W. REDMOND moved to leave out word "*Legislature*" and insert word "*Parliament.*"—(P.D., vol. XII., p. 493; T.D., vol. XXIV., p. 35.)

Mr. GLADSTONE opposed on ground that Colonial Assemblies were described as "Legislatures."—P.D., vol. XII., p. 495; T.D., vol. XXIV., p. 35.)

After an hour's discussion

The Committee divided—

| For the Amendment | ... | ... | 40 |
| Against the Amendment | | ... | 466 |

*(The Minority was made up of a few Radical and a certain number of the Irish Members.)

(Division List No. 75.)

Mr. T. W. RUSSELL moved (page 1, line 12) to leave out words :—

"*and of two Houses, the Legislative Council, and*"

He justified his action by the assertion that, although represented as a safeguard, the Unionists regarded the Second Chamber provided by the Bill as a sham. Under the second Schedule the Unionists would not have more than twenty votes.—(P.D., vol. XII., p. 526; T.D., vol. XXIV., p. 41.)

Mr. LABOUCHERE said he intended to vote as a matter of strategy. If he thought the House and the majority of the Members were in favour of one House instead of the proposed arrangement, he should certainly have pushed forward his own Amendment.—(P.D., vol. XII., p. 533 ; T.D., vol. XXIV., p. 42.)

Mr. DUNBAR BARTON, interrupted by Mr. Healy, suggested the latter should take part in the debate.

Mr. HEALY: "I am not such a fool."—(P.D., vol. XII., p. 535 ; T.D., vol. XXIV., p. 43.)

In the course of the debate Mr. Gladstone advocated a Second Chamber as a check and restraint.—(P.D., vol. XII., p. 553; T.D., vol. XXIV., p. 46.)

---

* RADICALS and the PARNELLITES.—The whole of the Anti-Parnellites voted with the Government, notwithstanding the presumed existence of Irish sentiment in favour of the "*restoration*" of Grattan's *Parliament*.

Mr. JUSTIN McCARTHY, in deference to British sentiment and Irish Unionist fears, gave a most cordial and ready acceptance to the proposal for a Second Chamber.—(P.D., vol. XII., p. 575; T.D., vol. XXIV., p. 49.)

Mr. BOYCE quoted Continental and American systems in favour of a Second Chamber, and pointed out that the vote on a Second Chamber would be remembered later.—(P.D., vol. XII., p. 588; T.D., vol. XXIV., p. 52.)

Mr. BALFOUR replied to this line of attack.—(P.D., vol. XII., p. 593; T.D., vol. XXIV., p. 53.)

Mr. ATHERLY JONES said this hint of Mr. Bryce's really hit off the Radical difficulty. The only reason why Irishmen put up with a Second Chamber was because they regarded it as a mere toy and plaything given to the Unionist Party.—(P.D., vol. XII., p. 601; T.D., vol. XXIV., p. 54.)

Mr. Saunders and Mr. Wallace (P.D., vol. XII., p. 604-5; T.D., vol. XXIV., p. 55,) amongst others took part in the debate.

On the question that the words "Two Houses" stand part of the Clause,

The Committee divided—

For the words	295
Against the words	244
Majority ...	51

(Division List No. 77.)

On the motion "that Clause I. stand part of the Bill,"

Mr. CHAMBERLAIN explained difficulty of opposition; there was no fair debate, and no amendments put down by Government;

and entire absence of information as regards the retention of members and finance. He further quoted Mr. Redmond on supremacy—(P.D., vol. XII., p. 685; T.D., p. 69;)—Mr. McCarthy on Sir Edward Reed's letter—(P.D., vol. XII., p. 686; T.D., p. 69;) —and Mr. W. O'Brien on "a measure of complete emancipation." —(P.D., vol. XII., p. 687; T.D., vol. XXIV., p. 70.)

Mr. Gladstone's reply to this speech set forth

(1) The admission that the adjustment of details, in the retention of members, was insurmountable; and

(2) The theory that Government had to wait on formation of public opinion before deciding line of policy.— (P.D., vol. XII., p. 689; T.D., vol. XXIV., p. 70.)

Sir JOHN RIGBY having contended that Parliament could not divest itself of its powers,

Sir JOHN GORST quoted an Act of 1791, passed for the purpose of setting at rest doubts as to the authority of the Imperial Parliament over Ireland, and a prior Act of 1783 dealing with a similar point.—(P.D., vol. XII., p. 792; T.D., vol. XXIV., p. 84.)

In the course of the debate—

Sir EDWARD REED said supremacy must be preserved by means of a clear and distinct clause.—P.D., vol. XII., p. 822; T.D., vol. XXIV., p. 91.)

He also referred to the rebellious and revolutionary state of mind of Irish members in the past, and said "wrongful acts done in the past remain wrongful acts still."—(P.D., vol. XII., p. 822; T.D., vol. XXIV., p. 91.)

The retention of Irish members to vote on all subjects would be playing false to the country, and the conditions under which the the Government had obtained support.—(P.D., vol. XII., p. 824, T.D., vol. XXIV., p. 92.)

Mr. T. H. BOLTON spoke of men on the Government benches prepared to vote for any measure at the bidding of their leaders.—(P.D., vol. XII., p. 830; T.D., vol. XXIV., p. 92.)

After a discussion of 8½ hours and the closure resolution,

The Committee divided—

For the Clause	...	...	...	...	309
Against the Clause	...	...	...	...	267
			Majority	...	42

(Division List No. 81.)

Clause II.

Powers of Irish Legislature.

2. With the exceptions and subject to the restrictions in this Act mentioned, there shall be granted to the Irish Legislature power to make laws for the peace, order, and good government of Ireland in respect of matters exclusively relating to Ireland or some part thereof.

The debate on this Clause extended over three days and occupied 20 hours. (May 15, 16, 17.)

Mr. **VICTOR CAVENDISH** moved to omit the words:—

"*with the exceptions and subject to the restrictions in this Act mentioned.*"—(P.D., vol. xii., p. 83; T.D. vol. xxiv., p. 93.)

Mr. CHAMBERLAIN asked for specific details as to what Irish Parliament could do?

Mr. GLADSTONE asked if the Government accepted the Amendment and consequent ones, would Mr. Chamberlain accept the Bill?

Mr. CHAMBERLAIN: "Certainly not."

Mr. GLADSTONE then replied to Mr. Chamberlain's queries. The Bill would hand over marriage law and factory legislation, but as regards standard of value in the matter of currency—no. Speaking generally they intended to resist limits to be imposed on concerns to be handed over to the Irish Parliament. He admitted the measure had in it something of the nature of an experiment.—(P.D., vol. XII., p. 939; T.D., vol. XXIV., p. 106.)

Mr. HENRY MATTHEWS said, under Bill, the Irish Government could make completely different code of criminal law.—(P.D., vol XII., p. 947; T.D., vol. XXIV., p. 108.)

Mr. STOREY announced he would vote for Amendment, because he had promised his constituents to vote for a Bill *with matters delegated specifically set out.*—(P.D., vol. XII., p. 963; T.D., vol. XXIV., p. 110.)

After three hours' discussion,

The Committee divided—

For the Amendment	228
Against the Amendment	275
Majority	47

(Division List No. 83.)

Mr. BARTLEY then moved to omit the words :—

"*subject to the restrictions*"

on the ground that the safeguards were a sham.—(P.D., vol. XII., p. 965; T.D., XXIV., p. 111.)

Mr. GLADSTONE, in reply, supported the restrictions by reference to the U.S. Constitution.—(P.D., vol. XII., p. 969; T.D., vol. XXIV., p. 111.)

The Amendment was by leave withdrawn.

Captain BETHELL moved Amendment to substitute the word "*delegated*" for "*granted.*"

A three-cornered Debate took place between Mr. Goschen, the Solicitor-General and Mr. Morley on the point.—(P.D., vol. XII., p. 981–6; T.D., vol. XXIV., p. 113–4.)

After half an hour's discussion and the closure resolution,

The Committee divided—

For the Amendment	186
Against the Amendment	251
Majority ...	65

(Division List No. 85.)

Mr. A. CROSS moved an Amendment giving the Irish Legislature power to make laws for :—

"*the making, maintaining, and improving of railways, tramways, canals, waterworks, reservoirs, gas and lighting works, fisheries, and all other things which are the subject matter of Bills known in either Houses of Parliament as Local Bills, and also for the confirmation of provisional orders.*"

[13

He contended it was one of the chief conditions of the Government position, that nothing should be given to Ireland that could not be given to Scotland—quoted Prime Minister on the point. (P.D.,vol. XII., p. 991 ; T.D., vol. XXIV., p. 114.)

Mr. GLADSTONE characterized the Amendment as "ludicrous."—(P.D., vol. XII., p. 994; T.D., vol. XXIV., p. 115.)

After an hour and a half's discussion,

The Committee divided—

For the Amendment	257
Against the Amendment	296
Majority ...	45

(Division List No. 86.)

Mr. BRODRICK moved to add at end of Clause:—

"*But it shall be lawful for Her Majesty, upon the address of both Houses of the Imperial Parliament, to diminish or restrain the whole, or any part of the powers therein granted to the Irish Legislature.*"

Mr. GLADSTONE opposed the Amendment, and, in a subsequent conversation with Mr. Balfour, said, the Bill did not create Executive powers although it created an Executive in appointing the Council of the Viceroy!—(P.D., vol. XII., p. 1063 ; T.D., vol. XXIV. p. 123.)

Sir EDWARD REED speaking later said, the Bill was being discussed under the "dangerous conditions" outlined by the Prime Minister in 1885.—(P.D., vol. XII., p. 1071 ; T.D., vol. XXIV., p. 126.)

Mr. T. W. RUSSELL, Mr. Blake, Mr. Ross and Mr. Arnold Forster spoke

After two hours' discussion and the closure resolution,

The Committee divided—
For the Amendment 247
Against the Amendment 303
Majority ... 56

(Division List No. 88.)

Sir **HENRY JAMES** moved to add at end of Clause:—

"*Provided that in the making of such laws, and in all matters pertaining to the carrying out of the powers conferred by this Act, both Houses shall, except as in this Act provided, have equal rights, powers, and privileges.*"

Mr. GLADSTONE said, Government might be disposed to accept first portion as to making of Laws, and suggested Amendment being held over till Clause XXXII. was reached.—(P.D. vol. XII., p. 1086; T.D., vol. XXIV., p. 128.)

Subsequently, in reply to Mr. Courtney, Mr. Gladstone said it was the intention to provide by Imperial enactment that there should be perfect and *bona fide* equality between the two chambers.—(P.D., vol. XII., p. 1087; T.D., vol. XXIV., p. 129.)

The Amendment was withdrawn.

Sir **HENRY JAMES** moved to add at end of Clause:—

"*Provided that notwithstanding anything in this Act contained the supreme power and authority of the Parliament of the United Kingdom of Great Britain and Ireland should remain unaffected and undiminished over all persons, matters and things within the Queen's dominions.*"

Mr. GLADSTONE, in accepting the spirit of the Amendment, suggested it should come later, in form of a new Clause.—(P.D., vol. XII., p. 1094; T.D., vol. XXIV., p. 131.)

In the debate which followed, Mr. Arthur Balfour, Mr. Morley, Mr. Courtney, Mr. Collings, Mr. Sexton, Mr. T. W. Russell, Sir Edward Clarke and others took part.

Mr. T. W. RUSSELL quoted Mr. Redmond in *Nineteenth Century* for October, 1892, and asked if the assertion in the Bill regarding Imperial Supremacy was part of the "Parliamentary compact" referred to in the words:—

"A Parliamentary compact would be entered into binding the Imperial Parliament to leave these rights dormant."— (P.D., vol. XII., p. 1106; T.D., vol. XXIV., p. 134.)

Mr. REDMOND: "No compact has been entered into with me."—(P.D., vol. XII., p. 1107; T.D., vol. XXIV., p. 134.)

Mr. CHAMBERLAIN quoted Mr. Redmond in August, 1892, in speech on Address in same spirit.—(P.D., vol. XII., p. 1120, 2—4; T.D., vol. XXIV., p. 136, 7.)

After three and a half hours' discussion,

Mr. GLADSTONE said:—"I am not in a position to resist the insertion of the words."—(P.D., vol. XII., p. 1127; T.D., vol. XXIV., p. 138.)

The Amendment was therefore agreed to.

Mr. GRANT LAWSON proposed to add at end:—

"*Provided that no such laws be repugnant to the law of Great Britain and Ireland.*"

After half an hour's discussion,

	The Committee divided—	
For the Amendment		215
Against the Amendment		265
	Majority	50

(Division List No. 89.)

On the motion, "That Clause II. as amended stand part of the Bill,"

Mr. BARTLEY opposed, and quoted Mr. Dillon, Mr. Davitt, and Mr. Healy as to their intentions when they obtained power.—(P.D, vol. XII., p. 1164,5; T.D., vol. XXIV., p. 142.)

Sir ASHMEAD BARTLETT, speaking later, drew from Mr. Gladstone the extraordinary statement that the concession regarding Imperial Supremacy was made on Second Reading!—(P.D., vol. XII., p. 1179; T.D., vol. XXIV., p. 144.)

Mr. FOWLER dealt with points regarding veto and supremacy. (P.D., vol. XII., p. 1190; T.D., vol. XXIV., p. 145.)

Mr. GRAHAM MURRAY argued there was nothing in the Bill to prevent *octroi* duties.—(P.D., vol. XII., p. 1195; T.D., vol. XXIV., p. 147.)

After two hours' discussion and the closure resolution,

	The Committee divided—	
For the Clause		287
Against the Clause		225
	Majority	62

(Division List No. 93.)

Mr. GOSCHEN then moved to report progress, and a discussion took place, in which grave complaints were made that Unionists were not given fair opportunity of reply.—(P.D., vol. XII., p. 1201; T.D., vol. XXIV., p. 140.)

Clause II.

[As Amended in Committee. The italics show the words added.]

With the exceptions and subject to the restrictions in this Act mentioned, there shall be granted to the Irish Legislature power to make laws for the peace, order, and good government of Ireland in respect of matters exclusively relating to Ireland or some part thereof. *Provided that, notwithstanding anything in this Act contained, the supreme power and authority of the Parliament of the United Kingdom of Great Britain and Ireland shall remain unaffected and undiminished over all persons, matters, and things within the Queen's dominions.*

Clause III.

3. The Irish Legislature shall not have power to make laws in respect of the following matters or any of them :—

(1.) The Crown, or the succession to the Crown, or a Regency; or the Lord Lieutenant as representative of the Crown; or

(2.) The making of peace or war or matters arising from a state of war; or

(3.) Naval or Military forces, or the defence of the realm; or

(4.) Treaties and other relations with foreign States or the relations between different parts of Her Majesty's dominions or offences connected with such treaties or relations; or

(5.) Dignities or titles of honour; or

(6.) Treason, treason-felony, alienage, or naturalization; or

(7.) Trade with any place out of Ireland; or quarantine, or navigation (except as respects inland waters and local health or harbour regulations); or

(8) Beacons, lighthouses, or sea marks (except so far as they can consistently with any general Act of Parliament be constructed or maintained by a local harbour authority); or

(9.) Coinage; legal tender; or the standard of weights and measures; or

(10). Trade marks, merchandise marks, copyright, or patent rights.

Any law made in contravention of this section shall be void.

The debates on this Clause extended over eleven sittings, and occupied 57 hours. (May 30, 31. June 1, 2, 5, 6, 7, 8, 9, 12, 13.)

Lord WOLMER moved—page 1, line 19—after "to" to insert:—
" *To discuss or pass resolutions or to* "

He quoted the fact that the great Irish vote in the States might use parties as a sort of battledore and shuttlecock, to obtain further concessions.—(P.D., vol. XII., p. 1574; T.D., vol. XXIV., p. 202.)

Mr. GLADSTONE replying said:—"In my opinion no course would be more unwise for the Committee to adopt than to make a declaration of power without having means to support it, I would ask the noble lord whether it is wise, not for the sake of the Irish Legislature, but for our own sake, to make prohibitions which we supply no means of enforcing.—(P.D., vol. XII., p. 1578; T.D., vol. XXIV., p. 204.)

Mr. BALFOUR, in dealing with Mr. Gladstone's opposition to the Amendment, quoted the Errington mission as a proceeding without consent, and without payment, by House of Commons.— (P.D., vol. XII., p. 1581; T.D., vol. XXIV., p. 205.)

Later, Mr. GLADSTONE replying to Mr. Balfour, said:—
"I refer the Right Hon. Gentleman to the 9th Clause, which it is our intention to propose and to do our best to induce the House to adopt."—(P.D., vol. XII., p. 1583; T.D., vol. XXIV., p. 205.)

Mr. CHAMBERLAIN said Mr. Gladstone had stated when he spoke of not allowing the Irish Parliament to take cognizance of matters other than those which are purely Irish, he only meant by Act,—that would be playing with the House, and, what was more important, it would be playing with the country.—(P.D., vol. XII., p. 1609; T.D., vol. XXIV., p. 210.)

The SOLICITOR-GENERAL "did not disguise the difficulties of the position." He did not deny that representatives could be sent to foreign powers, and that unauthorised utterances must necessarily bear weight.—(P.D., vol. XII., p. 1617; T.D., vol. XXIV., p. 212.)

After five hours' discussion

The Committee divided—

For the Amendment	238
Against the Amendment	259
Majority ...	21

(Division List No. 102.)

Lord WOLMER moved:—page 1, line 19—after "laws" to insert:—

> "*Or to entertain or grant votes in supply except on the recommendation of the Crown signified by a Minister of the Imperial Parliament.*"

Mr. Gladstone, Mr. Balfour, Sir Henry James, Mr. Collings and Mr. Chamberlain spoke.

After two and a half hours' discussion and the closure resolution,

The Committee divided—

For the Amendment	188
Against the Amendment	240
Majority	52

(Division List No. 103.)

A series of Amendments dealing with the question of Supremacy followed, but all were defeated.—(P.D., vol. XII., p. 1682, 90; T.D., vol. XXIV., p. 222, 7.)

Mr. BARTLEY proposed—page 2, line 1—after "forces" to insert:—

> "*or any police force other than a local police force required for local purposes and acting under the order of a local authority.*"

In the course of the Debate, Mr. Gladstone said he did not think the Irish Legislature ought to be in a position to recreate the Irish Constabulary. The force was abnormal in many of its conditions, and not lying within the proper attributes of a Local Legislature. Eventually he undertook to bring up words to meet the requirements of the case.

The Amendment was consequently negatived.

Mr. BYRNE moved—page 2, line 1—after "or" to insert :—

"*Carrying or using arms, armed associations and associations for drill or practice in the use of arms, or*"

Mr. SEXTON spoke warmly against the proposal, and complained of not being called upon to speak by the Chairman when he twice rose.—(P.D., vol. XIII., p. 65; T.D., vol. XXIV., p. 260.)

The Chairman and Mr. Gladstone apologised.—(P.D., vol. XIII., p. 68; T.D., vol. XIII., p. 260.)

Mr. GLADSTONE accepted Mr. Sexton's contention that it was unfair to cripple an Irish Legislature responsible for the "peace, order and good government of Ireland." He was however willing to insert words to prevent the creation of *quasi* military associations.—(P.D., vol. XIII., p. 69; T.D., vol. XXIV., p. 261.)

Mr. Wyndham, Colonel Saunderson, Mr. T. W. Russell, Mr. Courtney and Mr. Balfour spoke.

After two hours' discussion,

The Committee divided—

For the Amendment	245
Against the Amendment ...	283
Majority ...	38

(Division List No. 108.)

Mr. G. BALFOUR moved—page 2, line 5—after the word "or" to insert as a new sub-section the words :—

"(6.) *Appointment of Judges or Magistrates.*"

After a lengthy debate—(P.D., vol. xiii., p. 260–86; T.D., vol. XXIV., p. 289–95),

The Amendment was put with the words "mode of" before appointment,

The Committee divided—

For the Amendment	...	...	...	...	255
Against the Amendment		...	...	...	291
			Majority	..	36

(Division List No. 116.)

Mr. **BUTCHER** moved—page 2, line 6—after the word "treason-felony" to insert the words

"criminal conspiracy and combination."

A discussion took place, in which Mr. Gladstone charged Mr. Balfour with having "concocted" another law of conspiracy setting up new offences in connection with Act of 1887.—(P.D., vol. xiii., p. 344; T.D., vol. xxiv., p. 303.)

Mr. Morley, Mr. David Plunket, Mr. Dunbar Barton, Mr. Arnold Forster and others spoke.—(P.D., vol. xiii., p. 338-54; T.D., vol. xxiv., p. 300-4.)

After two hours' discussion and the Closure resolution,

The Committee divided—

For the Amendment	...	...	...	...	276
Against the Amendment		...	...	...	317
			Majority	...	41

(Division List No. 118).

Sir **HENRY JAMES** moved to add "*sedition*" after "treason-felony."

The Solicitor-General and Mr. Asquith spoke.—(P.D., vol. XIII., p. 354-61; T.D., vol. XXIV., p. 304-5.)

After three quarters of an hour's discussion,

The Committee divided—

For the Amendment	255
Against the Amendment	304
Majority ...	49

(Division List No. 119.)

Mr. STUART WORTLEY moved Amendments on "criminal conspiracy" and "Explosives," both of which were defeated.—(P.D., vol. XIII., p. 361-71; T.D., vol. XXIV., p. 305-307.)

Mr. BARTON, for **Mr. CARSON**, moved—page 2, line 6 — after words "treason-felony" to insert the words: -

"*procedure in criminal matters.*"

The Solicitor-General and Mr. Asquith opposed on the part of the Government. Mr. Carson, Sir Henry James, and Mr. Goschen spoke in favour of the Amendment.—(P.D., vol. XIII., p. 371-98; T.D., vol. XXIV., p. 307-12.)

After three hours' debate,

The Committee divided—

For the Amendment	253
Against the Amendment	293
Majority ...	40

(Divisional List, No. 121.)

Mr. BRODRICK moved—page 2, line 6—after the word "alienage" to insert the words—

"*the immigration and expulsion of aliens, the rights of aliens resident in Ireland.*"

There was quite a heated debate, in which Mr. Healy, Mr. Sexton, Mr. Blake, and Mr. W. Redmond protested.

After an hour and a half's discussion,

The Committee divided—

For the Amendment	328
Against the Amendment	139
Majority	189

Eventually the words "as such" were added on Mr. Sexton's motion.—(P.D., vol. XIII., p. 405-37; T.D., vol. XXIV., p. 313-18.)

---

*Mr. BARTLEY moved—page 2, line 7—to leave out the words "with any place out of Ireland," in order to insert the words:—

"*bounties to promote Irish Industries.*"

---

* It is to be noted that on this Amendment Mr. James Lowther (Thanet), as an avowed Protectionist, spoke and voted with the Government. Mr. Paul (Gladstonian member for Edinburgh) voted against the Government, whilst several other Gladstonian members walked out and did not vote.

Among the English members who voted for conferring on the Irish Parliament the power to give these bounties were:—Messrs. George Russell (Beds.), Halley Stewart (Spalding), Lambert (South Molton), Lawson (Cirencester), Logan (Harborough, Leicester), Luttrell (Tavistock), H. E. Hoare (Cambridgeshire), C. E. Hobhouse (Devises, Wilts.), Seale-Hayne (Ashburton, Devon), Billson (Barnstaple), Gardner (Saffron Walden), Arch (North-West Norfolk), Brand (Wisbech, Cambs.), Channing (East Northamptonshire), Cobb (Rugby), Conybeare (Camborne), Dodd (Maldon Division, Essex), and Sir Walter Foster (Ilkestone).—MR. JESSE COLLINGS, M.P. in *Rural World*.

[25

In the course of the debate—

Mr. CHAMBERLAIN quoted Mr. Morley in *Nineteenth Century* admitting Protectionist proclivities on part of Irish people.—(P.D., vol. XIII., p. 558; T.D. vol. XXIV., p. 334.)

Mr. GLADSTONE gave it as his opinion Irish Parliament would have power of dealing with premiums, and they ought to be within cognizance of Irish Parliament.—(P.D., vol. XIII., p. 563; T.D., vol. XXIV., p. 335.)

After a short discussion and closure resolution,

The Committee divided—

For the Amendment	252
Against the Amendment	288
Majority ...	36

(Division List No. 127.)

Mr. WHITELEY proposed—page 2, line 12,—after word "or" to insert as a new sub-section the words :—

"*Factories, workshops and mines, or the regulation of the hours of labour of men, women, and children in factories, workshops, and mines.*"

Sir JOHN GORST having referred to difficulty which would arise in consequence of Ireland sending representatives to labour conferences,

Mr. MUNDELLA advocated freedom in matter for Ireland.

Mr. RUSSELL challenged Irish Members to deny that the Irish people looked on Home Rule as a way to cheapen land and subsidise manufactures.—(P.D., vol. XIII., p. 664-5; T.D., vol. XXIV., p. 346-7.)

After two hours' discussion and the closure resolution,

The Committee divided—

For the Amendment	...	...	...	...	268
Against the Amendment		...	...	...	298
			Majority	...	30

(Division List No. 130.)

Sir JOHN LUBBOCK proposed—page 2, line 13—after the words "legal tender" to insert the words:—

"*banks, Bills of Exchange.*"

Mr. GLADSTONE admitted that bills drawn in Ireland on England would be Imperial, and in England on Ireland—local—*i.e.* treating Ireland as a foreign country.—(P.D., vol. XIII, p. 803; T.D., vol. XXIV., p. 365.)

Mr. GOSCHEN pointed out the arrangement would give different laws of exchange to each country forming a portion of the United Kingdom.—(P.D., vol. XIII., p. 815; T.D., vol. XXIV., p. 365.)

After an hour and three quarter's discussion,

The Committee divided—

For the Amendment	...	...	...	..	254
Against the Amendment		...	...	...	283
			Majority	...	29

(Division List No. 131.)

Sir F. S. POWELL proposed—page 2, line 16—after sub-section 10, to insert as a new sub-section:—

"(11) *Marriage and Divorce.*"

Mr. GLADSTONE opposed on grounds that American laws were of a very diversified character !—(P.D., vol. XIII., p. 848; T.D., vol. XXIV., p. 371.)

[27

LORD RANDOLPH CHURCHILL quoted differences of church laws in Ireland regarding marriage of first cousins, etc.— (P.D., vol. XIII., p. 856; T.D., vol. XXIV., p. 371.)

After an hour and three quarter's discussion.

The Committee divided—

For the Amendment	...	...	236
Against the Amendment		...	270
	Majority	...	34

(Division List No. 133.)

Clause III., as amended, was then passed.

Clause III.

[As Amended in Committee. The italics show the words added. The words in black type bracketed were deleted.]

The Irish Legislature shall not have power to make laws in respect of the following matters or any of them :—

(1.) The Crown, or the succession to the Crown, or a Regency; or the Lord Lieutenant as representative of the Crown; or

(2.) The making of peace or war or matters arising from a state of war; *the regulation of the conduct of any portion of Her Majesty's subjects during the existence of hostilities between foreign states with which Her Majesty is at peace, in respect of such hostilities;* or

(3.) **[Naval or military forces, or the defence of the realm, or]** *Navy, army, militia, volunteers, and any other military forces, or the defence of the realm or forts, permanent military camps, magazines, arsenals, dockyards, and other needful buildings, or any places purchased for the erection thereof;* or

(4.) Treaties and other relations with foreign States, or the relations between different parts of Her Majesty's dominions, or offences connected with such treaties or relations, *or procedure connected with the extradition of criminals under any treaty*; or

(5.) Dignities or titles of honour; or

(6.) Treason, treason-felony, alienage, *aliens as such*, or naturalization; or

(7.) Trade with any place out of Ireland; or quarantine, or navigation, *including merchant shipping* (except as respects inland waters and local health or harbour regulations); or

(8.) *Lighthouses, buoys, or beacons within the meaning of the Merchant Shipping Act*, 1854 [**beacons, lighthouses, or sea marks**] (except so far as they can consistently with any general Act of Parliament be constructed or maintained by a local harbour authority) ; or

(9.) Coinage; legal tender; or *any change in* the standard of weights and measures; or

(10) Trade marks, merchandise marks, copyright, or patent rights.

Provided always, that nothing in this section shall prevent the passing of any Irish Act to provide for any charges imposed by Act of Parliament.

It is hereby declared that the exceptions from the powers of the Irish Legislature contained in this section are set forth and enumerated for greater certainty, and not so as to restrict the generality of the limitation imposed in the previous section on the powers of the Irish Legislature.

Any law made in contravention of this section shall be void.

Clause IV.

4. The powers of the Irish Legislature shall not extend to the making of any law—

(1.) Respecting the establishment or endowment of religion, or prohibiting the free exercise thereof; or

(2.) Imposing any disability, or conferring any privilege, on account of religious belief; or

(3.) Abrogating or prejudicially affecting the right to establish or maintain any place of denominational education or any denominational institution or charity; or

(4.) Prejudicially affecting the right of any child to attend a school receiving public money, without attending the religious instruction at that school; or

(5.) Whereby any person may be deprived of life, liberty or property without due process of law, or may be denied the equal protection of the laws, or whereby private property may be taken without just compensation; or

(6.) Whereby any existing corporation incorporated by Royal Charter or by any local or general Act of Parliament (not being a corporation raising for public purposes taxes, rates cess, dues, or tolls, or administering funds so raised) may, unless it consents, or the leave of Her Majesty is first obtained on address from the two Houses of the Irish Legislature, be deprived of its rights, privileges, or property without due process of law; or

(7.) Whereby any inhabitant of the United Kingdom may be deprived of equal rights as respects public sea fisheries.

Any law made in contravention of this section shall be void.

The debate on this Clause extended over nine sittings, and lasted 52½ hours. (June 13, 14, 15, 16, 19, 20, 21, 22, 23).

Mr. GRIFFITH BOSCAWEN proposed—page 2. line 23—after the word "belief" to insert:—

"*or political opinions.*"

A discussion took place regarding the attack made upon the Bank of Ireland by the "*Freeman's Journal.*"

Mr. WILLIAM KENNY contended the attack was because of the Unionist character of the Directors.—(P.D., VOL. XIII., p. 955; T.D. XXIV., p. 387.)

Mr. CLANCY had contended previously that the attack was to get publication of balance sheets, but now Mr. HARRINGTON gave an entirely different version, and said in addition to a desire to arrange for the obtaining of the site for a College Green Parliament (the Bank was the old Irish House of Commons), the owner of the *Freeman* was interested in a rival Bank and was glad of an opportunity of attack.—(P.D., vol. XII, p. 958; T.D. vol. XXIV., p. 388). (NOTE.—In *Times* Mr. Harrington's remarks are attributed to Mr. T. P. O'Connor.)

Mr. KENNY also quoted procedure adopted by *Freeman's Journal* with regard to "black list" of those merchants who attended the Balfour Banquet in Dublin; and the language of the *Irish Independent* of 31st March, 1893, with regard to the enemies of Ireland.—(P.D., vol. XIII. p. 955-6; T. D., vol. XXIV., p. 388.)

Mr. BALFOUR quoted Mr. W. O'Brien in *Speaker* on clearing out the Castle.—(P.D., vol. XIII., p. 960; T.D., vol. XXIV., p. 388.)

Mr. CHAMBERLAIN quoted Mr. Dillon on "ruffianly magistrates and Policemen."—(P.D., vol. XIII., p. 970; T.D., vol. XXIV., p. 390.)

After about an hour and half's discussion,

The Committee divided—

For the Amendment	233
Against the Amendment	269
Majority	36

(Division List No. 138.)

Mr. VICARY GIBBS proposed—page 2, after line 26—to insert:—

> *"Imposing any new desirability or conferring any new privilege on any Institution belonging to or conducted by any religious denomination or"*

In the discussion Mr. SEXTON asked if it was seriously proposed to withdraw from the Irish Legislature the task of completing the provision for University Education in Ireland, without regard to the question whether it should be carried out or not in the interests of a particular section of the community.

Mr. ARTHUR BALFOUR said his reply was quite direct and simple. He should not leave to the Irish Legislature the power of taxing Protestants and Catholics alike for the purpose of establishing a denominational place of education.—(P.D., vol. XIII., p. 1,009; T.D., vol. XXV., p. 398.)

The Amendment being of too wide a character was withdrawn.

Mr. MOWBRAY moved—page 2, line 30—after "whereby," to insert:—

> *"the privileges or immunities of any of Her Majesty's subjects in the United Kingdom may be abridged or whereby"*

It was pointed out that these words were left out while the context of them was taken from the American Constitution—

In reply to Lord Wolmer,

The ATTORNEY-GENERAL said:— "There were cases in which the Irish Government would have, and cases where they would not have the power of suspending the Habeas Corpus."—(P.D., vol. XIII., p. 1101; T.D., vol. XXIV., p. 412.)

In reply to Mr. Chamberlain,

The ATTORNEY-GENERAL said:—" Sub-section five did not in all cases preserve the right to trial by jury."—(P.D., vol XIII., p. 1106; T.D., vol. XXIV., p. 413.)

After two hours' discussion,

The Committee divided—

For the Amendment	...	...	...	...	208
Against the Amendment	...	...	...	249
			Majority	...	41

(Division List No. 144.)

Mr. SETON-KARR then moved—page 2, line 31—to leave out:—

"*without due process of law.*"

In the discussion—

The Attorney-General explained the Irish Government could pass an Act making it a crime to take part in a party procession and impose fine or imprisonment. It could not pass an Act making every occupier of Irish land an owner in fee simple; it could make sheep stealing a capital offence. The Habeas Corpus could be suspended where there was an emergency or circumstances requiring such action.—(P.D., vol. XIII., p. 1115; T.D., vol. XXIV., p. 415.)

The Amendment was then withdrawn.

A discussion took place regarding the proper interpretation of the words, "due process of law," in which Mr. Wyndham, Mr. Bolton, the Solicitor-General, Mr. Barton, Mr. Arthur Balfour, Sir Henry James, the Attorney-General, Sir Edward Clarke, Mr. Chamberlain, Mr. Bryce and others took part.—(P.D., vol. XIII., p. 1130-54; T.D., vol. XXIV., p. 416, 23.)

As the result of the foregoing discussion Mr. Gerald Balfour brought in an Amendment,—page 2, line 31,—after "law" to insert:—

> "*in accordance with the settled principles and precedents of judicial procedure unalterable save by the Parliament of the United Kingdom.*"

He quoted the opinions given by the Attorney-General and Solicitor-General, as to their view of the words being expressed by the terms of amendment.—(P.D., vol. XIII., p. 1199; T.D., vol. XXIV., p. 426.)

Eventually the Amendment was worded in the following form:—

> "*in accordance with settled principles and precedents.*"

Mr. SEXTON sought to have "regard being had to" substituted for "in accordance with." He gave expression to the significant remark that language used in debate is one thing, and that language to be inserted in a Clause in the form of a definition was another.—(P.D., vol. XIII., p. 1207; T.D., vol. XXIV., p 427.)

After an hour's debate

The Committee divided—
For Mr. Sexton's Amendment 144
Against Mr. Sexton's Amendment ... 324
Majority ... 180

The Unionist Party thus saved the Government from defeat at the hands of the Irish members.—(Division List No. 146.)

Mr. CLANCY and Mr. SEXTON then made a bitter attack on the Government.—(P.D., vol. XIII., p. 1213-16; T.P., vol. XXIV., p. 428-9.)

                The Committee again divided—
    For the Amendment   310
    Against the Amendment   165
                    Majority   ...   145

The Unionist Party and the Government again voted together, the Irish Party being joined by a certain portion of the Radical section.—(P.D., vol. XIII., p. 1218; T.D., vol. XXIV., p. 429; Division List No. 147.)

Mr. H. PLUNKETT moved—page 2, line 1.—after the word "law" to insert:—

> "*or any person not otherwise provided for in this Act be deprived of any office or situation which such person may have occupied on the appointed day.*"

Mr. Morley, Mr. Sexton, Mr. Balfour, Mr. W. Redmond and Mr. T. W. Russell having spoken,

Mr. CLANCY said—"This was a point on which the Irish Members would admit of no concession."—(P.D., vol. XIII., p. 1238; T.D., vol. XXIV., p. 432.)

Mr. CHAMBERLAIN drew attention to the significance of the phrase as shewing the Irish mastery of the Government.

After an hour's discussion,

            The Committee divided—
    For the Amendment   211
    Against the Amendment   253
                    Majority   ...   44

(Division List No. 149.)

Mr. T. H. BOLTON moved—page 2, line 33—after "taken," to insert:—

"*or injuriously affected,*"

The ATTORNEY-GENERAL said "the section did not exhaust every possible case that could occur."

Mr. BALFOUR commented on the fact that heretofore the debate had been conducted on an assumption which was the exact opposite, *i.e.*, that the Clauses III. and IV. gave a concise, full and accurate description of all an Irish Parliament could not do. *They had been misled up to now*, 19*th June.* Now the Attorney-General refused to accept an amendment with which he agreed.— (P.D., vol. XIII., p. 1361; T.D., vol. XXIV., p. 440.)

After an hour's discussion,

The Committee divided—

For the Amendment	250
Against the Amendment	284
Majority ...	34

(Division List No. 151.)

Mr. RENTOUL moved—page 2, line 33—at end to insert:—

"*Suspending or prejudicially affecting the right of any person to the writ of* habeas corpus."

The ATTORNEY-GENERAL in opposing "could not rise to the level of the hon. gentleman's fears" with regard to the possible action respecting Ulster. Why should not the Irish Parliament have the power of doing what the Imperial Parliament had frequently done? This Bill was to relieve Parliament of Irish legislation.—(P.D. vol. XIII., p. 1391; T.D., vol. XXIV., p. 452.)

Sir Henry James, Mr. Gladstone, and Lord Randolph Churchill took part in the debate, in the course of which it was pointed out that the constitution of the United States prevents a State from suspending *habeas corpus* unless for rebellion or invasion. The powers which the United States Government *did not give* to the several States Legislatures *were proposed to be given to Ireland;* and it was argued that such tremendous powers should not be given to any subordinate Parliament of the Crown, but should remain in the hands of the Parliament of the United Kingdom.

It was further pointed out that the Government candidates had pledged themselves at the election to protect the minorities in Ireland, whereas now the Irish Government was to be allowed to mark down any opponents and imprison them without trial.—(P.D., vol. XIII., p. 1392—1409; T.D., vol. XXIV., p. 453—457.)

After two and a half hours' discussion

The Committee divided—

For the Amendment	241
Against the Amendment	270
Majority ...	29

(Division List No. 154.)

Lord WOLMER proposed—page 2, line 33, at end to insert:—

"(6) *of an ex post facto character.*"

He pointed out such provision existed in the American Constitution.

The ATTORNEY-GENERAL *denied the likelihood of the Irish Legislature doing anything wrong.*—(P.D., vol. XIII., p. 1505; T.D., vol. XXIV., p. 466.)

Mr. CHAMBERLAIN quoted Mr. Dillon on "when they came out of the struggle."—(P.D., vol. XIII., p. 1510; T.D., XXIV., p. 467.)

Mr. Haldane, Mr. W. Balfour, Mr. Gladstone and Sir Henry James spoke.

After an hour and a half's discussion

The Committee divided—

For the Amendment	240
Against the Amendment	270
Majority	30

(Division List No. 156.)

Lord WOLMER moved—page 2, line 33—at end to insert:—

"*impairing the obligation of contracts or.*"

He quoted American Constitution to show how these words were taken from it, and also Mr. O'Brien and Mr. Davitt on "prairie value."—(P.D., vol. XIII., p. 1525; T.D., vol. XXIV., p. 470.)

Mr. RATHBONE moved as an **Amendment to the Amendment** to add:—

"*Except with the consent of Parliament testified by an address to Her Majesty from both Houses of Parliament.*"

He said "till the country had settled down and come to understand what was possible by legislation, he believed it would be impossible even by as powerful a man as Mr. Parnell himself was, to pass legislation without making promises, which could not be carried out; and on this ground he thought a provision such as the modified one he ventured to recommend to the House would be invaluable."

The ATTORNEY-GENERAL in reply stated the view of the Government. If at the end of the three years referred to in Clause XXXV. the land question remained unsettled, the Imperial Parliament would be under the obligation of fixing the terms and conditions under which it would delegate the power to deal with it to the Irish body.—(P.D., vol. XIII, p. 1531; T.D., vol. XXIV., p. 471.)

In reply to Mr. Balfour,

The ATTORNEY-GENERAL said if Clause XXXV. was inapt for the purpose indicated, it might be necessary to make some alteration.—(*Ibid.*)

Mr. Arnold Forster, Mr. Carson and Mr. Morley having spoken,

Mr. CHAMBERLAIN quoted Lord Spencer on the Land Question.—(P.D. vol. XIII., p. 1547; T.D., vol. XXIV., p. 474).

The debate was continued amidst much interruption from the Irish Benches.

After three and a half hours' discussion
        The Committee divided—

For the Amendment (as amended)	223
Against the Amendment (as amended) ...	260
Majority ...	37

(Division List No. 157.)

Mr. PARKER SMITH moved—line 2, page 33—after the word "or" to insert the words:—

"(6) *Whereby any censorship of the Press shall be established or a public meeting for legal purpose shall be interfered with.*"

Mr. SEXTON made a violent speech against the Amendment, and charged the Opposition with obstruction, "reducing the House of Commons to a state of impotence," whereupon

Mr. BUCKNILL quoted Mr. Sexton on Second Reading, where *he undertook the acceptance of all restrictions* calculated to allay apprehension even where unfounded.—(P.D., vol. XIII., p. 1576; T.D., vol. XXIV., p. 480.)

The Amendment was put and negatived without a Division.

[39

Mr. DAVID PLUNKET moved—line 2, page 33—after the word " or " to insert as a new sub-section the words:—

"(6) *affecting the constitution, endowment, prosperity, or privileges of Trinity College, Dublin, or of the Universities of Dublin or.*"

He instanced the case that 20 years ago one of the strongest Governments that ever existed in England was defeated in the attempt to reconcile within the University of Dublin, the demand made by the Irish Roman Catholic prelates. The system of education had been denounced by them as a danger to the faith and morals of the people. He also quoted Dr. Walsh on the subject in 1886.—(P.D., vol. XIII., p. 1580-90; T.D., vol. XXIV., p. 481, 3.)

Mr. GLADSTONE contended the safeguards were sufficient. To establish a precedent like this in regard to one institution would be most undesirable and unfair.

Mr. SEXTON contended that neither Archbishop, prelate nor any other Bishop considered the disturbance of Trinity College too essential to settlement of University Question.

Mr. CARSON quoted Archbishop Logue in 1873—that Queen's College and University of Dublin were "Godless institutions," and dangerous to the faith of Catholic students.—(P.D., vol. XIII., p. 1596; T.D., vol. XXIV., p. 485.)

Mr. John Redmond, Mr. Courtney, Mr. Ross, Mr. Balfour, Mr. Sexton, Mr. Goschen, Mr. T. W. Russell, Sir A. Rollitt also spoke, in addition to

Mr. W. KENNY, who pointed out that in the Bill of 1886, the Government did what they now objected to do by Amendment— (P.D., vol. XIII., p. 1610; T.D., vol. XXIV., p. 486)—and Mr. Harrington, who quoted several statements by Archbishop Walsh.—(P.D., vol. XIII., p. 1614; T.D. vol. XXIV., p. 487.)

On the understanding that Mr. Balfour's question as to whether or not the Irish Legislature could establish a Roman Catholic

University under the Clause, would be dealt with and answered when the whole Clause was before the House.—(P.D., vol. XIII., p. 1622; T.D., vol. XXIV., p. 488.)

After three and a half hours' discussion,

The Committee divided—

For the Amendment 242
Against the Amendment 284

Majority 42

(Division List No. 160.)

NOTE.—*See Mr. Plunket's Amendment later.*

A discussion took place regarding the wording of sub-section 4. which

The ATTORNEY-GENERAL admitted needed some alteration, and which he undertook to bring up altered on report.—(P.D., vol. XIII., p. 1689-96; T.D., vol. XXV., p. 497.)

Mr. D. PLUNKET moved—page 2, line 39—after the word "*Legislature*" to insert:—

"*And after a copy of the proposed law has lain for not less than forty days on the table of both Houses of Parliament*"—

He asked for acceptance of this Amendment because of Prime Minister's statement respecting Trinity College.

The ATTORNEY-GENERAL thought the Prime Minister must have been misunderstood.

Mr. PLUNKET quoted the Prime Minister, shewing they were to have a three-fold protection against unfair treatment—

(1.) The consent of the Corporation was to be obtained.

(2.) The consent of the Irish Legislature.

(3.) The *locus standi* of the Imperial Parliament to interfere —hence the words of the Amendment.

(P.D., vol. XIII., p. 1699-1702 ; T.D., vol. XXIV., p. 498, 9.)

The discussion turned on the question as to whether the action of the Government now, in Mr. Gladstone's absence, refusing to support his undertaking did not suggest the view that the vote of the previous day had been **obtained** under false pretences.

Sir Henry James, the Solicitor-General, Mr. Carson, Mr. A. Balfour, Mr. Asquith, Mr. Goschen, Mr. Sexton and Mr. Courtney spoke.

After an hour's discussion,

The Committee divided—
For the Amendment	261
Against the Amendment	307
Majority	46

(Division List No. 163.)

Mr. **COCHRANE** proposed—page 2, line 41—to insert :—

"*whereby any undue preference, benefit or advantage is given to or conferred directly or indirectly upon any person or body of persons, class, body corporate, or institution, or*"

He quoted Mr. Bryce on Religious persecution, and Mr. Gladstone's admission on the possibility of giving indirect preference to one denomination over another.—(P.D., vol. XIII., p. 1718; T.D., vol. XXIV., p. 500.)

Mr. MORLEY suggested adding some such words "or by imposing any liability or conferring any privilege, benefit or advantage on any subject of the Crown, on account of present age or place of birth or upon any Corporation or Institution carrying on its operations in the land on account of the person by whom or in whose favour such operations are carried."—(P.D., vol. XIII., p. 1722; T.D., vol. XXIV., p. 500.)

Mr. CLANCY strongly objected, and said this addition went further than the Nationalists had ever been prepared to concede. They should oppose it when the time came.—(P.D., vol. XIII., p. 1729; T.D., vol. XXIV., p. 502.)

Mr. Chamberlain, Sir Henry James, Mr. A. Balfour, Colonel Nolan, Mr. Heneage and Mr. MacFarlane also spoke.

Leave to withdraw the original Amendment was withheld, and after an hour and half's discussion,

The Committee divided—

For the Amendment	... 218
Against the Amendment	... 260
Majority	... 42

(Division List No. 164.)

Mr. COCHRANE, on behalf of Lord Randolph Churchill, moved :—page 2, line 4—after sub-section (6) to insert :—

> "*whereby any voluntary institution, association or society lawfully constituted according to the laws of the United Kingdom in force for the time being is prejudicially affected*"

The Amendment it was explained was designed for the protection of the Freemasons. They numbered some 9,000 or 10,000, and possessed valuable property in the way of schools. Mr. Cochrane quoted Archbishop Walsh : *The Catholic* of

3rd June, 1893: and read a letter from "Lawrence Burke," of the Abbey, Roscommon, 6th June, 1893, in which the rites of burial were refused in consequence of Freemasonry.—(P.D., vol. XIII., p. 1738-41; T.D., vol. X., XXIV., p. 503-4.)

Mr. GLADSTONE objected on grounds that Amendment would prevent Irish Government dealing with case like the Balfour Liberator Society, and because the Government conscientiously and emphatically refused "to cast suspicion of such a gross offence in the teeth of the Irish Members."—(P.D., vol. XIII., p. 1742-3; T.D., vol. XXIV., p. 504.)

After three-quarters of an hour's debate and the Closure Resolution.

The Committee divided—

For the Amendment	243
Against the Amendment	278
Majority ...	35

(Division List No. 166.)

Mr. PARKER SMITH moved—page 2, line 41—to insert as a new section:—

> "(7) *Whereby the actions of any official of the Government shall be removed from the cognizance of the ordinary law or*"

He pointed out that the design was to prevent the Irish Government from adopting the system of "*droit administratif*" by which Continental officials were rendered secure from actions.

Mr. MORLEY refused because "it would not be likely" that the Irish Government *would* resort to the practice.—(P.D., vol. XIII., p. 1790; T.D., vol. XXIV., p. 511.)

Mr. CHAMBERLAIN pointed out that Mr. Morley could not possibly speak for any future body of Irish Legislators.

The Committee divided—

For the Amendment		230
Against the Amendment		272
Majority		42

(Division List No. 168.)

On the Question "that Clause IV., as amended, stand part of the Bill,"

Mr. BALFOUR asked for the promised information on the Education Question.

Mr. GLADSTONE said—"(1) the Government accepted training colleges as within the provisions of the Clause, and (2) what amounted to endowment or was open to the charge of preference could not be done by the Irish Legislature; but he was not prepared to say that all collegiate education of a denominational character, if it were accompanied by certain conditions, was excluded by the Bill. *The foundation of a Roman Catholic College was therefore possible..*"—(P.D., vol. XIII., p. 1602-3; T.D., vol. XXIV., p. 513-14.)

Mr. CHAMBERLAIN called attention to the fact that it was only now at the end of twenty days in Committee they became acquainted with the fact that the Irish Government would be empowered to subsidise a Roman Catholic College at the expense of the Irish Protestants. The safeguards would be considered worthless.

Mr. R. WALLACE again spoke on the retention of members. —(P.D., vol. XIII., p. 1811-18; T.D., XXIV., p. 515-17.)

Lord Randolph Churchill, Mr. Morley, Mr. T. W. Russell and Mr. Goschen spoke, and subsequently

The CLAUSE, as amended, was added to the Bill.

Clause IV.

[*As Amended in Committee. The italics show the words added. The words in black type bracketed were deleted.*]

The powers of the Irish Legislature shall not extend to the making of any law:—

(1.) Respecting the establishment or endowment of religion, *whether directly or indirectly*, or prohibiting the free exercise thereof; or

(2.) Imposing any disability, or conferring any privilege, *advantage, or benefit*, on account of religious belief; or

(3.) *Diverting the property of any religious body*, abrogating or prejudicially affecting the right to establish or maintain any place of denominational education or any denominational institution or charity; or

(4.) Prejudicially affecting the right of any child to attend a school receiving public money, without attending the religious instruction at that school; or

(5.) Whereby any person may be deprived of life, liberty, or property without due process of law *in accordance with settled principles and precedents*, or may be denied the equal protection of the laws, or whereby private property may be taken without just compensation; or

(6.) Whereby any existing corporation incorporated by Royal Charter or by any local or general Act of Parliament (not being a corporation raising for public purposes taxes, rates, cess, dues, or tolls, or administering funds so raised) may, unless it consents, or the leave of Her Majesty is first obtained on address from the two Houses of the Irish Legislature, be deprived of its rights, privileges, or property without due process of law *in accordance with settled principles and precedents*; ; or

(7.) [**Whereby any inhabitant of the United Kingdom may be deprived of equal rights as respects public sea fisheries.**]

Any law made in contravention of this section shall be void.

Clauses V.—VIII.

FIRST COMPARTMENT.

Executive Authority.

5.—(1.) The executive power in Ireland shall continue vested in Her Majesty the Queen, and the Lord Lieutenant, on behalf of Her Majesty, shall exercise any prerogatives or other executive power of the Queen, the exercise of which may be delegated to him by Her Majesty, and shall, in Her Majesty's name, summon, prorogue, and dissolve the Irish Legislature.

(2.) There shall be an Executive Committee of the Privy Council of Ireland to aid and advise in the Government of Ireland, being of such numbers, and comprising persons holding such offices, as Her Majesty may think fit, or as may be directed by Irish Act.

(3.) The Lord Lieutenant shall, on the advice of the said Executive Committee, give or withhold the assent of Her Majesty to Bills passed by the two Houses of the Irish Legislature, subject, nevertheless, to any instructions given by Her Majesty in respect of any such Bill.

The debate on this Clause [V.] extended over five days and had occupied 31 hours, when the "Gag" was employed. (June 28, July 3, 4, 5, 6.)

Mr. HAYES FISHER moved—page 3, line 6—after "Lieutenant" to insert:—

"*or other chief executive officer or officers for the time being appointed in his place.*"

After a short debate in which the Government refused the Amendment, the question was put a second time, and the Government suddenly changed front and accepted the addition.'

[47

Mr. HANBURY moved—page 3, line 6—after the words "Lord Lieutenant" to leave out the words "on behalf of Her Majesty," and insert:—

> "*with the approval of Her Majesty, signified by a Secretary of State.*"

Mr. BRYCE admitted that the proposed Irish Legislature would differ from Grattan's Parliament, as in the latter the Executive was not responsible to the Irish Parliament.—(P.D., vol. XIV., p. 255; T.D., vol. XXIV., p. 5557.)

Mr. BALFOUR commented on the length of the Rt. Hon. Gentleman's speech in view of the threatened "Gag."

After three hours' discussion

The Committee divided—

For the Amendment	... 231
Against the Amendment	... 260
Majority	... 29

(P.D., vol. XXIV., p.   ; Division List No. 172.)

It was at this point that the "Gag" Resolutions were discussed and adopted as follows:—

"That the proceedings in Committee on the Government of Ireland Bill, unless previously disposed of, shall at the times hereinafter mentioned be brought to a conclusion in the manner hereinafter mentioned:—

> (*a.*) "The proceedings on the Clauses V. to VIII., both inclusive, not later than 10 p.m. on Thursday, 6th July;
>
> (*b.*) "The proceedings on Clauses IX. to XXVI., both inclusive, not later than 10 p.m. on Thursday, 13th July;

(*c.*) The proceedings on Clauses XXVII. to XL., both inclusive, not later than 10 p.m. on Thursday, 20th July;

(*d.*) The proceedings on the postponed clauses, new clauses, being Government clauses, schedules, and preamble not later than 10 p.m. on Thursday, 27th July; and after the clauses, schedules, and preamble are disposed of, the Chairman shall forthwith report the Bill, as amended, to the House.

Then at the said appointed times the Chairman shall put forthwith the question or questions on any amendment or motion already proposed from the Chair.

He shall next proceed, unless and until progress be moved as hereinafter provided, successively to put forthwith the following questions:—

That any clause or schedule then under consideration, and any of the said clauses or schedules not already disposed of, stand part of, or be added to, the Bill.

After the passing of this order no dilatory motion, nor motion to postpone a clause, shall be received unless moved by a Minister in charge of the Bill, and the question on any such motion shall be put forthwith; if progress be reported the Chairman shall put this order in force in any subsequent sitting of the Committee; proceedings under this order shall not be interrupted under the provisions of any standing order relating to the sittings of the House."

Lord WOLMER moved—page 3, line 10—after Sub-section 1, to insert:—

(1.) "*For the due enforcement of any decision of the Civil Council or of any Act of Parliament, the Lord-Lieutenant acting under instructions from Her Majesty may appoint in each County of Ireland so many officers as he may deem necessary for the purpose, who shall be entitled in Ireland to all privileges, immunities, and powers which a sheriff possesses by law."*

In the course of the discussion, Mr. Chamberlain repeated a quotation he had previously made from a speech of Mr. Dillon of a criminatory character. Mr. Dillon, in reply, stated that he made the quotation while in a state of indignation with reference to the affray at Mitchelstown. Mr. Chamberlain pointed out that the Mitchelstown incident did not occur until nearly a year afterwards.

Mr. HARRINGTON followed with reference to the Chamberlain-Duignan correspondence.

After two hours' discussion,

The Committee divided—
For the Amendment 196
Against the Amendment 230

Majority ... 34

(Division List No. 186.)

Mr. BRODRICK proposed—page 3, line 10, after sub-section (1)—to insert:—

"*The Lord-Lieutenant shall not exercise any of the prerogatives or powers the exercise of which may be delegated to him by Her Majesty in furtherance of or in connection with any of the matters with regard to which the Irish Legislature has not power to make laws, save so far as may be necessary to carry out any existing law or future Act of Parliament, including this Act.*"

Mr. MORLEY in reply to various questions explained when the Lord-Lieutenant wanted advice on different matters he would consult the heads of the different English departments, as for instance in a case of treason the referee would be the Home

Secretary or English Attorney-General.—(P.D., vol. XIV., p. 755; T.D., vol. XXIV., p. 621.)

Mr. GOSCHEN described this as not a revelation of a plan but a revelation of chaos. Who was to give instructions to the Lord-Lieutenant.?

Mr. MORLEY. The Home Office, no doubt.

Mr. GOSCHEN said the Lord-Lieutenant was to have three capacities, Imperial, Irish and hybrid, with the constabulary under his management advised by the Irish Government. (Mr. Morley had just stated the Constabulary would not be regarded as Imperial.)

Mr. MORLEY explained the Home Secretary would draw up instructions, but details of operations would be left to the Lord-Lieutenant.

Mr. GOSCHEN said this would be on all fours with the present arrangement, save, that the Chief Secretary who would be replaced by the Lord-Lieutenant in this regard, was open to criticism on the votes, but the Lord-Lieutenant would not be.—(P.D., vol. XIV., p. 757-8; T.D., vol. XXIV., p. 621.)

Replying to Mr. Courtenay,

Mr. MORLEY said, what he meant was that the Home Secretary could be called to account for the action of the Lord-Lieutenant.—(P.D., vol. XIV., p. 762; T.D vol. XXIV., p. 622.)

Mr. BALFOUR pointed out Mr. Morley and Mr. Bryce were at variance in regard to the matter.

Questioned regarding what would happen in the event of a resignation of the Irish Ministry.

Mr. MORLEY said the Lord-Lieutenant would act on his own not on the Imperial Cabinet's responsibility in summoning a new Cabinet.—(P.D, vol. XIV., p. 767; T.D., vol. XXIV., p. 624.)

[51

After about four hours' discussion,

    The Committee divided—
For the Amendment	247
Against the Amendment	274
Majority	27

(Division List No. 1876.)

A heated discussion took place on an Amendment by Mr. Arnold Forster dealing with the prerogative of mercy.—(P.D., vol. XIV., p. 826-52; T.D., vol. XXIV., p. 631-75.)

The MARQUIS OF CARMARTHEN moved to leave out the words:—

   "*or as may be directed by this Act.*"

Mr. D. PLUNKET drew attention to the change from the Bill of '86, which read "by the aid of such advisers and such Council as Her Majesty may from time to time seem fit."—(P.D., vol. XIV., 878; T.D., vol. XXIV., p. 641.)

Mr. AMBROSE said to pass the sub-section as it stood would be *suicidal to the supremacy of Great Britain*.—(P.D., XIV., p. 907; T.D., XXIV., p. 642.)

The Amendment was eventually withdrawn.

An interesting discussion, regarding the worth of the Veto, took place on an Amendment, by Lord Wolmer, to leave out the words "on the advice of the said 'Executive Committee.'"—(P.D., vol. XIV., p. 978-1006; T.D., vol. XXIV., p. 652-6.)

After the rejection of several Amendments

  The "Gag" was applied at ten o'clock.

    The Committee divided—
For the Clause	324
Against the Clause	289
Majority	35

(Division List No. 198.)

⁂ Clauses VI., VII., and VIII., were then passed without discussion.

(*See Division Lists, Nos.* 199, 200.)

Clause V.

[As Amended in Committee. The italics show the words added.]

(1.) The executive power in Ireland shall continue vested in Her Majesty the Queen, and the Lord Lieutenant, *or other chief executive officer or officers for the time being appointed in his place*, on behalf of Her Majesty, shall exercise any prerogatives or other executive power of the Queen the exercise of which may be delegated to him by Her Majesty, and shall, in Her Majesty's name, summon, prorogue, and dissolve the Irish Legislature; *and every instrument conveying any such delegation of any prerogative or other executive power shall be presented to the two Houses of Parliament as soon as conveniently may be.*

(2.) There shall be an Executive Committee of the Privy Council of Ireland to aid and advise in the Government of Ireland being of such numbers, and comprising persons holding such offices *under the Crown* as Her Majesty may think fit, or as may be directed by Irish Act.

(3.) The Lord Lieutenant shall, on the advice of the said Executive Committee, give or withhold the assent of Her Majesty to Bills passed by the two Houses of the Irish Legislature, subject nevertheless to any instructions given by Her Majesty in respect of any such Bill.

---

* In the division on Clause 6 ten Gladstonians voted with the Opposition—Sir C. Dilke, Dr. Clark, Dr. Wallace, Messrs. W. Allen, Atherley-Jones, Burns, Conybeare, Kearley, Labouchere, and Storey. The Government majority would have been still further reduced but for the fact that Mr. Beckett was unable to reach the House in time to take part in the division, being delayed through the congestion of traffic in the streets. Mr. Benn was the Gladstonian member who paired with Mr. Villiers after the adoption of Clause 6, but through a misunderstanding he voted with the Government, in the division on Clause 7. His mistake having been pointed out to him, he did his best to make the *amende honorable* by voting with the Opposition on Clause 8.—*Times*, Political Notes, 7th July.

[53

Clauses VI., VII., and VIII., not altered in Committee.

(July 6.)

Clauses IX.—XXVI.

SECOND COMPARTMENT.

Irish Representation in House of Commons.

9. Unless and until Parliament otherwise determines, the following provisions shall have effect—

(1.) After *the appointed day* each of the constituencies named in the Second Schedule to this Act shall return to serve in Parliament the number of members named opposite thereto in that schedule, and no more, and Dublin University shall cease to return any member.

(2.) The existing divisions of the constituencies shall, save as provided in that schedule, be abolished.

(3.) An Irish representative peer in the House of Lords and a member of the House of Commons for an Irish constituency shall not be entitled to deliberate or vote on—

(a) any Bill or motion in relation thereto, the operation of which Bill or motion is confined to Great Britain or some part thereof; or

(b) any motion or resolution relating solely to some tax not raised or to be raised in Ireland; or

(c) any vote or appropriation of money made exclusively for some service not mentioned in the Third Schedule to this Act ; or

(d) any motion or resolution exclusively affecting Great Britain or some part thereof or some local authority or some person or thing therein ; or

(e) any motion or resolution, incidental to any such motion or resolution as either is last mentioned, or relates solely to some tax not raised or be raised in Ireland, or incidental to any such vote or appropriation of money as aforesaid.

(4.) Compliance with the provisions of this section shall not be questioned otherwise than in each House in manner provided by the House.

(5.) The election laws and the laws relating to the qualification of parliamentary electors shall not, so far as they relate to parliamentary elections, be altered by the Irish Legislature, but this enactment shall not prevent the Irish Legislature from dealing with any officers concerned with the issue of writs of election, and if any officers are so dealt with, it shall be lawful for Her Majesty by Order in Council to arrange for the issue of such writs, and the writs issued in pursuance of such Order shall be of the same effect as if issued in manner heretofore accustomed.

The Debate on this Clause extended over five sittings and occupied 261½ hours, when the "Gag" was applied. (July 7, 10, 11, 12, 13.)

***Mr. JOHN REDMOND** moved to leave out Sub-section 1. He quoted Mr. Parnell in 1886 in denial of the assertion that this

---

* In the division on Mr. John Redmond's Amendment seven Parnellites—Messrs. J. Redmond, W. Redmond, Clancy, Field, Maguire, Hayden, and Colonel Nolan—voted against the Government; as did Mr. Labouchere. Sir Charles Dilke took no part in the division.—*Times* Political Notes, July 11th.

[55

question of retention was a purely English matter, and explained that his (Mr. Redmond's) amendment was a protest against the reduction to eighty.—(P.D., vol. XIV., p. 1168; T.D., vol. XXIV., p. 682.)

Mr. GLADSTONE, in reply, said he did not agree that the Irish Parliament was going to be deprived of all essential powers during that period (six years). The land question was not reserved for six years, and the honourable gentleman surely did not suppose that that question could be dealt with during the first three years by an Irish Parliament.—(P.D., vol. XIV., p. 1172; T.D., vol. XXIV., p. 682.)

A long discussion took place as to what a vote on the Amendment would pledge the Committee to.

Eventually the Committee divided—

For the Amendment	266
Against the Amendment	280
Majority	14

(Division List No. 204.)

---

*Mr. HENEAGE moved—page 4, line 27—to leave out from "day" to end of Sub-section II.:—

> "*Ireland shall cease to return members to the House of Commons, and the persons who on the said day are such members shall cease to be members of the House of Commons.*"

He quoted Mr. Gladstone in 1886.—(P.D., vol. XIV., p. 1196; T.D., vol. XXIV., p. 687.)

---

* There was no cross-voting in the division on Mr. Heneage's Amendment, and the smallness of the Government majority was, therefore, due entirely to Gladstonian absenteeism. In the closure division Mr. J. A. Bright, finding himself compelled to take part in the voting, although paired, went into the Government lobby. Most of the Gladstonian members who were expected to support the Amendment abstained.—*Times*, Political Notes, 11th July.

Mr. CHAPLIN quoted Mr. Morley, 7th January, 1885, on "order in Ireland and power in the House of Commons."— (P.D., vol. XIV., p. 1199; T.D., vol. XXIV., p. 688.)

Mr. WINGFIELD DIGBY quoted Mr. Fowler in 1891; Sir Charles Russell's definition of Home Rule; and Mr. Shaw Lefevre on the necessity of carrying Home Rule by a large majority.— (P.D., vol. XIV., p. 1206; T.D., vol. XXIV., p. 689.)

Sir William Harcourt, Colonel Saunderson, Mr. Carson, and Mr. Wyndham spoke.

Mr. CHAMBERLAIN quoted Mr. Gladstone at Swansea, in 1887, on retention being a British question on which Great Britain should have a determining voice; Lord Rosebery on the "in and out" question; also Sir George Trevelyan on the worthlessness of the veto under the circumstances; and Mr. Morley on the real strength of the position; and *United Ireland* on the general situation.—(P.D., vol. XIV., p. 1229-35; T.D., vol. XXIV., p. 693-5.)

Mr. BALFOUR quoted Mr. Morley at Newcastle, in 1886, on "the arbitrators and masters of English policy." etc.—(P.D., vol. XIV., p. 1,243; T.D., vol. XXIV., p. 696.)

After four and a half hours' discussion and the closure resolution,

The Committee divided—	
For the Amendment	209
Against the Amendment	240
Majority ...	31

(Division List No. 206.)

Sir JOHN LUBBOCK moved—page 4, line 27—after the the word "day" to insert:—

"*Existing Constituencies shall be abolished, and a number of members shall be returned from Ireland to serve in Parlia-*

ment bearing the same proportion to the total number of members as the contribution of Ireland fixed in this Act bears to the total Imperial expenditure."

He pointed out that under the Bill Ireland, speaking roughly, would bear 1-40th of the burden—why should she have 5-40ths of the power? The proportion of payment would be 6/6 for every Irishman against 35/- for every Englishman and Scotchman.—(P.D., vol. XIV., p. 1288-9; T.D., vol. XXIV., p. 701.)

The Amendment was negatived.

Sir **CHARLES DILKE** proposed—page 4, line 27—after the word "constituencies" to insert the word "*hereinafter.*"

Mr. GLADSTONE, in opposing, described the scheme as being "in the rough." The Government had proceeded on a basis which would avoid disfranchisement. Later on, when twitted with the admission by Mr. Goschen, Mr. Gladstone denied having made it.—(P.D., vol. XIV., p. 1308; T.D., vol. XXIV., p. 705.)

Mr. RUSSELL gave some examples of the injustice of the method employed.—(P.D., vol. XIV., p. 1309; T.D., vol. XXIV., p. 705.)

In the course of the debate there was constant misrepresentation of the Chairman's ruling with regard to Mr. Redmond's motion, from the Government benches. Lord Randolph Churchill called attention to the fact that under the ruling the Opposition had to vote with Mr. Redmond as the only way in which the exclusion of members could be raised. Now it was being contended that because the Opposition had voted in this way, every attempt to amend the Clause in other directions was a direct departure from principle.—(P.D., vol. XIV., p. 1314; T.D., vol. XXIV., p. 706.)

Mr. JOHN REDMOND said by the vote on his Amendment *some scheme of redistribution was necessary, but the present was imperfect.*—(P.D., vol. XIV., p. 1316; T.D. vol. XXIV, p. 707.)

After two hours' discussion,

The Committee divided—

For the Amendment ...	...	... 182
Against the Amendment	...	... 212
Majority	...	30

(Division List No. 207.)

In the course of further discussion—

Mr. BARTLEY called attention to the fact that although Dr. Wallace had most emphatically protested against any Irish Members being retained, he had voted for the retention of 80.—(P.D., vol. XIV., p. 1330; T.D., vol. XXIV., p. 709.)

Mr. JOHN REDMOND announced his intention to vote for University representation in order to increase the number of Irish representatives.—(P.D., vol. XIV., p. 1364; T.D. vol. XXIV., p. 71.)

Mr. DAVID PLUNKET spoke of the general character of University representation.—(P.D., vol. XIV., p. 1382; T.D. vol. XXIV., p. 7187.)

On the eve of the adjournment on Wednesday, 12th July, the day previous to the "gagging" of the second compartment, and *when only some five hours remained for discussion,*

Mr. GLADSTONE moved the omission of Sections III. and IV. of the Clause under discussion [IX.]—(P.D., vol. XIV., p. 25; T.D., vol. xxiv., p. 725.)

Mr. RATHBONE protested.—(P.D., vol. XIV., p. 1425; T.D., vol. XXIV., p. 727.)

Mr. WALLACE followed in a humorous speech, which was

[59

delivered in two Sittings.—(P.D., vol. XIV., p. 1427 and 1486; T.D., vol. XXIV., p. 728 and 735.)

Mr. LABOUCHERE thought the best plan was total exclusion.—(P.D., vol. XIV., p. 1495; T.D., vol. XXIV., p. 738.)

Later on, in reply to Mr. Balfour, he explained he would not vote in support of this conviction for fear of wrecking the Bill.—(P.D., vol. XXIV., p. 1502; T.D., XXIV., p. 739.)

Mr. BALFOUR having spoken and been replied to in a heated speech by Mr. Gladstone,

Mr. CHAMBERLAIN quoted Mr. Gladstone's previous references to retention. He challenged Mr. Gladstone with direct evasion and refusal to declare the Government policy on the matter.

Mr. GLADSTONE:—"I fully understood the purport of the questions of my right honourable friend, and I was determined to defeat it."—(P.D., vol. XIV., p. 1519; T.D., vol. XXIV., p. 744.)

Sir William Harcourt, Mr. Darling. Mr. John Redmond, Sir Henry James and Mr. Atherly Jones, spoke in addition to Dr. Clark, who said he could not support the change of policy. If the Government went to the Country with this they would go to certain defeat.—(P.D., vol. XIV., p. 1535; T.D., vol, XXIV., p. 747.)

The "Gag" was applied at 10 o'clock.

The Committee divided—

For the Omission	325
Against the Omission...	298
Majority	27

On the motion that the Clause be added

The Committee divided—

For the Clause	326
Against the Clause	297
Majority	29

(Division Lists 211–212.)

Clause IX.

As Amended in Committee. The italics show the words added. The words in black type bracketed were deleted.]

Unless and until Parliament otherwise determines, the following provisions shall have effect :—

(1.) After the appointed day each of the constituencies named in the Second Schedule to this Act shall return to serve in Parliament the number of members named opposite thereto in that Schedule, and no more, and Dublin University shall cease to return any member.

(2.) The existing divisions of the constituencies shall, save as provided in that Schedule, be abolished.

[(3.) **An Irish representative peer in the House of Lords and a member of the House of Commons for an Irish constituency shall not be entitled to deliberate or vote on—**

(*a*) any Bill or motion in relation thereto, the operation of which Bill or motion is confined to Great Britain or some part thereof; or

(*b*) any motion or resolution relating solely to some tax not raised or to be raised in Ireland; or

(*c*) any vote or appropriation of money made exclusively for some service not mentioned in the Third Schedule to this Act; or

(*d*) any motion or resolution exclusively affecting Great Britain or some part thereof or some local authority or some person or thing therein; or

(*e*) any motion or resolution, incidental to any such motion or resolution as either is last mentioned, or relates solely to some tax not raised or be raised in Ireland, or incidental to any such vote or appropriation of money as aforesaid.

(4.) **Compliance with the provisions of this section shall not be questioned otherwise than in each House in manner provided by the House.**]

(3.) The election laws and the laws relating to the qualification of parliamentary electors shall not, so far as they relate to parliamentary elections, be altered by the Irish Legislature, but this enactment shall not prevent the Irish Legislature from dealing with any officers concerned with the issue of writs of election, and if any officers are so dealt with, it shall be lawful for Her Majesty by Order in Council to arrange for the issue of such writs, and the writs issued in pursuance of such Order shall be of the same effect as if issued in manner heretofore accustomed.

Clauses X., XI., XII., XIII., XVII., XX., XXI. were then put and negatived without discussion.

Clauses XIV., XV., XVI. were postponed.

Clauses XVIII., XIX., XX., XXII., XXIII., XXIV., XXV., XXVI. were put and adopted without discussion.

(Division Lists 213-20.) (July 13.)

---

* The series of divisions which took place last night under the second compartment of the "guillotine" resolution was devoid of exciting incident. The cross-voting on Clause 9, was in consequence of the extreme pressure brought to bear upon the Gladstonian Waverers by the party wire-pullers, less than had been anticipated; and upon the subsequent Clauses the dissent did not assume a more serious form than occasional abstentions. Five Gladstonians— Mr. Bolton, Mr. Wallace, Mr. Rathbone, Mr. Atherly-Jones, and Dr. Clark—voted against the Government on Mr. Gladstone's Amendment to Clause 9; and two—Messrs. C. E. Shaw and Illingworth—abstained. In the second division, however—on the question that Clause 9 as amended stand part of the Bill— Messrs. Shaw and Illingworth supported the Government, while Mr. Wallace abstained. The Unionist "Whipping" was magnificent, nearly every member being accounted for either in the division lists or in the list of pairs. Even Mr. Villiers, the "father of the House," put in an appearance, and took part in the first two divisions. After Clause 9 had been disposed of he left, but not until a pair had been found for him.—*Times* Political Notes.

Clauses XXVII.—XL.

THIRD COMPARTMENT.

Government of Ireland.

27.—(1.) All existing judges of the Supreme Court, county court judges, and Land Commissioners in Ireland and all existing officers serving in Ireland in the permanent civil service of the Crown and receiving salaries charged on the Consolidated Fund of the United Kingdom, shall, if they are removable at present on address from both Houses of Parliament, continue to be removable only upon such address, and if removable in any other manner shall continue to be removable only in the same manner as heretofore; and shall continue to receive the same salaries, gratuities, and pensions, and to be liable to perform the same duties as heretofore, or such duties as Her Majesty may declare to be analogous, and their salaries and pensions, if and so far as not paid out of the Irish Consolidated Fund, shall be paid out of the Exchequer of the United Kingdom : Provided that this section shall be subject to the provisions of this Act with respect to the Exchequer judges.

(2.) *If any of the said judges, commissioners, or officers retires from office with the Queen's approbation before completion of the period of service entitling him to a pension, Her Majesty may, if she thinks fit, grant to him such pension, not exceeding the pension to which he would on that completion have been entitled, as to Her Majesty seems meet.*

The debates on this Clause extended over one sitting, and lasted six and a half hours. (July 17.)

Mr. **SEXTON** moved—page 15, line 21—to omit :—

"*and Land Commissioners of Ireland.*"

Mr. MORLEY, in the course of replies to different members,

said the purpose of the Clause was simply "to protect vested interests." The question as to the purchase money and laws affecting the same would be found dealt with in the Financial Clauses, but so long as money was advanced out of British Treasury the Irish Parliament would not be able to alter or vary conditions of advance.—(P.D., vol. XIV., p. 1719; T.D., vol. XXV., p. 6.)

The Amendment was by leave withdrawn later on.

Mr. STOREY spoke of "a sordid policy," and advocated Irish Government being free to transfer officers or get rid of them on the best terms in the public interest.

Mr. SETON-KARR pointed out that Mr. Storey should not take exception to this as a sordid policy, inasmuch as he was one of those who wanted to appropriate public funds for payment of members.—(P.D. vol. XIV., p. 1740; T.D. vol. XXV., p. 8).

Mr. CHAMBERLAIN asked what security would British taxpayers have for repayment if Civil Service salaries were to be on British Exchequer guarantee.

Mr. Morley and Mr. Sexton replied—Clause XIV.

Mr. GOSCHEN regarded this as most unsatisfactory. The Lord-Lieutenant might sign a cheque, but how was it to be honoured?—(P.D., vol. XIV., p. 1743; T.D., vol. XXIV., p. 9.)

Mr. MORLEY proposed—page 15, line 21—at end of Clause, as a new sub-section, to add the words:—

> "*This section shall apply to existing officers serving in the permanent Civil Service of the Crown who, although receiving salaries out of money provided by* **Parliament**, *are removable only for misconduct or incapacity.*"

THE BILL IN COMMITTEE.

Mr. SEXTON proposed to insert at beginning of the Amendment:—

"*Sub-section* 1 *of.*"

Mr. MORLEY having intimated agreement with Mr. Sexton's view,

Mr. SETON-KARR complained he had been led to withdraw a previous Amendment in the interests of the Clerks of the Crown, in the belief that the Government represented themselves as in sympathy with its spirit; and now another Amendment of the very opposite character was being accepted. *He charged a breach of faith with the Committee.*—(P.D., vol. XIV., p. 1755; T.D., vol. XXV., p. 10.)

Mr. WM. KENNY said there were three classes of Civil Servants provided for under the 27th and 28th Clauses: (1) those whose salaries were charged on the Consolidated Fund; (2) those who held office during good behaviour; (3) those who held during pleasure, and whose salaries were not charged on Consolidated Fund. But for Mr. Morley's Amendment the second class would have come under the 28th Clause. The Bankruptcy Judges were of the third class. How were they to be treated? Why should not they get the benefit of the full clause? It was not accurate to represent the present Amendment as framed to meet an inadvertence. The Government intention, set forth in April last, was quite clear, and pointed to giving those latter officers all the benefits.—(P.D., vol. XIV., p. 1759; T.D., vol. XXV., p. 11.)

After an hour and a half's discussion,

The Committee divided—

For Mr. Sexton's Amendment	...	...	194
Against the Amendment	...	...	142
	Majority	...	52

(Division List No. 221.)

Mr. T. W. RUSSELL moved to add at the end of Sub-section :—

"*And Sub-section II. shall apply to the Judges in Bankruptcy.*"

After a short discussion Mr. Morley undertook to deal with the matter on report.

(P.D., vol. XIV., 1774; T.D., vol. XXV., p. 13.)

Mr. SETON-KARR moved to add at the end of the Clause the following sub-sections :—

"*The Superannuation Act, 1859 (the 22nd year of Victoria, chapter 26, section 4), shall be deemed to extend to the office of clerks of the Crown and peace appointed under the County Officers and Courts (Ireland) Act, 1877, and every such officer on retiring shall be entitled on the computation of the amount of his superannuation allowance to have added to the number of years he may have actually served a further additional 15 years on account of professional or other peculiar qualifications not ordinarily to be acquired in the public service, and every such officer shall be entitled to such superannuation after a period of service of five years.*

"*In case the said office of clerk of the Crown and peace be abolished, every existing officer, if then holding office, shall be entitled to a superannuation allowance equal to his three-fourths salary, such allowance to be payable out of the Exchequer of the United Kingdom.*"

Mr. BALFOUR pointed out that by the acceptance of Mr. Sexton's Amendment the Civil Servants had been divided into two classes—one to receive, and the other to be excluded, from the benefits of Sub-section II. He suggested they should now divide on this Amendment, and reserve discussion on general retirement until Clause XXVIII.

The Committee divided—

For the Amendment	201
Against the Amendment	246
Majority	45

(Division List No. 222.)

Clause XXVII.—As amended, No. XXIV.

[*As Amended in Committee. The italics show the words added. The words in black type bracketed were deleted.*]

(1.) All existing judges of the Supreme Court, county court judges, and Land Commissioners in Ireland and all existing officers serving in Ireland in the permanent civil service of the Crown and receiving salaries charged on the Consolidated Fund of the United Kingdom, shall, if they are removable at present on address from both Houses of Parliament, continue to be removable only upon such address, and if removable in any other manner shall continue to be removable only in the same manner as heretofore; and shall continue to receive the same salaries, gratuities, and pensions, and to be liable to perform the same duties as heretofore, or such duties as Her Majesty may declare to be analogous, and their salaries and pensions [**if and so far as not paid out of the Irish Consolidated Fund**] shall be paid out of the Exchequer of the United Kingdom, *and all sums so paid shall be repaid to that Exchequer from the Irish Exchequer:* Provided that this section shall be subject to the provisions of this Act with respect to the Exchequer judges.

(2.) If any of the said judges, commissioners, or officers retires from office with the Queen's approbation before completion of the period of service entitling him to a pension, Her Majesty may, if she thinks fit, grant to him such pension not exceeding the pension to which he would on that completion have been entitled, as to Her Majesty seems meet.

(3.) *Sub-section* (1) *of this section shall apply to existing officers serving in Ireland in the permanent civil service of the Crown, who, although receiving salaries out of money provided by Parliament, are removable only for misconduct or incapacity.*

CLAUSE XXVIII.

28.—(1.) All existing officers in the permanent civil service of the crown, who are not above provided for, and are at the appointed day serving in Ireland, shall after that day continue to hold their offices by the same tenure and to receive the same salaries, gratuities, and pensions, and to be liable to perform the same duties as heretofore or such duties as the Treasury may declare to be analogous; *and the said gratuities and pensions, and until three years after the passing of this Act, the salaries due to any of the said officers if remaining in his existing office, shall be paid to the payees by the Treasury out of the Exchequer of the United Kingdom.*

(2.) Any such officer may after *three years* from the passing of this Act retire from office, and shall, at any time during those three years, if required by the Irish Government, retire from office, and on any such retirement may be awarded by the Treasury a gratuity or pension in accordance with the Fifth Schedule to this Act; Provided that—

(*a*) six months' written notice shall, unless it is otherwise agreed, be given either by the said officer or by the Irish Government as the case requires; and

(*b*) such number of officers only shall retire at one time and at such intervals of time as the Treasury, in communication with the Irish Government, sanction.

(3.) If any such officer does not so retire, the Treasury may award him after the said three years a pension in accordance with the Fifth Schedule to this Act, which shall become payable to him on his ultimate retirement from the service of the Crown.

5 (4.) *The gratuities and pensions awarded in accordance with the Fifth Schedule to this Act shall be paid by the Treasury to the payees out of the Exchequer of the United Kingdom.*

(5.) All sums paid out of the Exchequer of the United Kingdom in pursuance of this section shall be repaid to that Exchequer
10 from the Irish Exchequer.

(6.) This section shall not apply to officers retained in the service of the Government of the United Kingdom.

The debate on this Clause extended over three sittings, and lasted 13½ hours. (July 17, 18, 19.)

Mr. MORLEY explained the scheme and the scope of the clauses at some length.—(P.D., vol. XIV., p. 1779; T.D., vol. XXV., p. 14.)

Mr. BALFOUR and Mr. GLADSTONE dealt with the possibilities of change and the attitude of the Irish Members towards Civil Service, &c.—(P.D,, vol. XIV., p. 1841–59; T.D., vol. XXV., p. 21–24.)

Dealing with Mr. GLADSTONE'S contention that in addition to following the English principle of adding a certain number of years to service to produce increase of pension, the Government credited the Irish Civil Servant with the five years of the transitional period, although he might not have served that time,— Mr. GOSCHEN said :—" Only in certain cases. The officers who have not served their full time may be benefited, but those who serve the full five years receive no benefit at all from the arrangement."

Mr. GLADSTONE :—" Does my right honourable friend see that they have not chosen to take advantage of the provision ? They can give six months' notice ; and if they choose to do so, four and a half years out of the five will be enjoyed by every one of them."   [69

Mr. GOSCHEN :—By sacrificing four and a half years' salary, they get five years' half salary.—(P.D., vol. XIV., p. 1854; T.D., vol. XXV., p. 23.)

Mr. T. W. RUSSELL called attention to the fact that the Irish Members had frequently threatened to clear out the Irish Land Commissioners at the first opportunity. He quoted case of clerk with 13 years' service receiving £170 per annum and a pension of £91 13s. 4d. In the natural course this man, at the end of his service, would realize £6,095. Another clerk, with 12 years' service, £170 per annum and pension of £88 would realize £6,428. Then, as regards their liabilities, one of them paid house rent of £40, life insurance of £12, and was a married man with a young family. Was it fair to leave it to the Irish Government to dismiss these men?—(P.D. vol. XIV., p. 1867; T.D. vol. XXV., p. 25.)

At the end of a lengthy and detailed discussion the Clause as amended was added to the Bill.

Clause XXVIII.—No. XXV. as amended.

[*As Amended in Committee. The italics show the words added. The words in black type bracketed were deleted.*]

(1.) All existing officers in the permanent civil service of the Crown, who are not above provided for, and are at the appointed day serving in Ireland, shall after that day continue to hold their offices by the same tenure and to receive the same salaries, gratuities, and pensions *according to the scale of the class to which they belong*, and to be liable to perform the same duties as heretofore or such duties as the Treasury *in communication with the Irish Government* may declare to be analogous; *and during the period of five years after the passing of this Act (in this section and the Fourth Schedule referred to as the transitional period,)* the said gratuities and pensions, [**and until three years after the passing of this Act, the salaries due to any of the said officers, if remaining in his existing office**] shall be [**paid** to the payees] *awarded by the Treasury after communicating with the Irish Government, and the gratuities and pensions so awarded and the said salaries shall be paid to the payees* by the Treasury out of the Exchequer of the United Kingdom. *Any such officer shall during the transitional period hold office unless he—*

[(2.) **Any such officer may after three years from the passing of this Act retire from office, and shall, at any time during those three years, if required by the Irish Government, retire from office, and on any such retirement may be awarded by the Treasury a gratuity or pension in accordance with the Fifth Schedule to this Act; Provided that—**]

(*a.*) *leaves the service on a medical certificate, or under the existing rules as to age, or is dismissed for misconduct or incapacity; or*

(*b.*) *is removed upon an abolition of office or re-organization of department which does not involve the appointment of any new officer; or*

(*c.*) *resigns under this section; or*

(*d.*) *is required by the Irish Government to retire.*

Provided that—

(*a.*) six months' written notice *of resignation under this section or of required retirement* shall, unless it is otherwise agreed, be given either by the said officer or by the Irish Government as the case requires; and

(*b.*) *before the end of the transitional period* such number of officers only shall *resign under this section, or be required to* retire at one time and at such intervals of time as the Treasury, *after* [**in**] communication with the Irish Government, sanctions, *however that a notice to resign under this section given by an officer shall, unless withdrawn, operate at the end of the transitional period if he has not sooner left the service; and*

[(3.) **If any such officer does not so retire, the Treasury may award him after the said three years a** pension in accordance with the Fifth Schedule to this Act, which shall become payable to him on his ultimate retirement from the service of the Crown.]

(c.) *an officer resigning under this section shall show that he is not incapacitated by mental or bodily infirmity for the performance of his duties, and that he will not be required under the existing rules as to age to retire before the end of the transitional period, and otherwise he shall not be entitled to any further gratuity or pension than he would have been entitled to if he had left the service on a medical certificate.*

(3.) *Upon any such removal, or resignation under this section, or required retirement, there may be awarded to the officer by the Treasury, after communication with the Irish Government, a gratuity or pension in accordance with the Fourth Schedule to this Act, and for that purpose his service shall be reckoned as if it had continued to the end of the transitional period, or to any earlier date at which under the existing rules as to age he will be required to retire.*

[(4.) The gratuities and pensions awarded in accordance with the Fifth Schedule to this Act shall be paid by the Treasury to the payees out of the Exchequer of the United Kingdom.]

(4.) *If any such officer is serving in a capacity which qualifies him for a pension under the Superannuation Act, 1859, and continues to hold office after the end of the transitional period the Treasury may, within three months after the end of that period, award him a pension in accordance with the Fourth Schedule to this Act which shall become payable to him on his ultimate retirement from the service of the Crown.*

(4.) *The gratuities and pensions awarded in pursuance of this section, shall be paid by the Treasury to the payees out of the Exchequer of the United Kingdom.*

(5.) All sums paid out of the Exchequer of the United Kingdom in pursuance of this section shall be repaid to that Exchequer from the Irish Exchequer.

(6.) This section shall not apply to officers retained in the service of the Government of the United Kingdom, *except that this section shall apply to the Clerical staff of the Royal Irish Constabulary and Dublin Metropolitan Police, with the substitution of the Treasury for the Irish Government.*

(7.) *Where an officer, though not in the permanent civil service, is in the public service of the Crown, then—*

(a.) *if he devotes his whole time to the duties of his office, this section shall apply to him in like manner as if he were in the permanent civil service; and*

(b.) *if he does not so devote his whole time, and is removed from his office for any cause other than incapacity or misconduct, he may apply to the Treasury, who may award him compensation for loss of office in accordance with the Fifth Schedule to this Act.*

(8.) *This section shall apply to petty sessions clerks and to officers in the registry of petty sessions clerks in like manner as to officers in the public service of the Crown, with the exceptions that any payment in pursuance of this section to any such clerk or officer shall be made out of the fund out of which the pension of such clerk or officer is payable instead of out of the Exchequer of the United Kingdom, and that in considering the amount of gratuity or pension regard shall be had to the amount of the fund;*

Provided that—

(a.) *If, by reason of anything done after the appointed day, the fund becomes insufficient to meet the full amount of the said gratuities and pensions, the deficiency shall be charged on and paid out of the Irish Consolidated Fund, but such charge shall be repaid, if and when the state of the fund allows to the Irish Consolidated Fund; and*

(b.) *the existing accumulated fund shall not be applied for any new purpose until every such gratuity and pension is satisfied.*

(9.) *For the purpose of determining finally the facts on all questions which may arise during the transitional period, as to the rights of the officers or any of them under this section, there shall be appointed a committee, consisting* of *A. B., the chairman, and C. D., and one other person to be nominated after the appointed by the Executive Committee of the Irish Privy Council. Any vacancy which may arise among the persons named in this section, may be filled by Her Majesty under Her Royal Sign Manual, and any vacancy which may arise from the death or resignation of the person nominated by the Executive Committee may be filled by that Committee.*

Clause XXIX.

29. Any existing pension granted on account of service in Ireland as a judge of the Supreme Court or of any court consolidated into that court, or as a county court judge, or in any other judicial position, or as an officer in the permanent civil service of the Crown other than in an office the holder of which is after the appointed day retained in the service of the Government of the United Kingdom, shall be charged on the Irish Consolidated Fund, and if and so far as not paid out of that fund, shall be paid out of the Exchequer of the United Kingdom.

The Clause was agreed to with verbal alteration without debate. (July 19.)

Clause XXX.

Police.

30.—(1.) The forces of the Royal Irish Constabulary and Dublin Metropolitan Police shall, when and as local police forces are from time to time established in Ireland in accordance with the Sixth

Schedule to this Act, be gradually reduced and ultimately cease to exist as mentioned in that Schedule ; and after the passing of this Act, no officer or man shall be appointed to either of those forces ;

Provided that until the expiration of *six* years from the appointed day, nothing in this Act shall require the Lord-Lieutenant to cause either of the said forces to cease to exist, if as representing Her Majesty the Queen he considers it inexpedient.

(2.) The said two forces shall, while they continue, be subject to the control of the Lord-Lieutenant as representing Her Majesty, and the members thereof shall continue to receive the same salaries, gratuities, and pensions, and hold their appointments on the same tenure as heretofore, *and those salaries, gratuities, and pensions, and all the expenditure incidental to either force, shall be paid out of the Exchequer of the United Kingdom.*

(3.) When any existing member of either force retires under the provisions of the Sixth Schedule to this Act, the Treasury may award to him a gratuity or pension in accordance with that Schedule.

(4.) *Those gratuities and pensions and all existing pensions payable in respect of service in either force, shall be paid by the Treasury to the payees out of the Exchequer of the United Kingdom.*

(5.) *Two-thirds of the net amount payable in pursuance of this section out of the Exchequer of the United Kingdom shall be repaid to that Exchequer from the Irish Exchequer.*

The debate on this Clause extended over one sitting and lasted $5\frac{1}{2}$ hours. (July 20.)

Mr. BOLTON moved—page 16, line 24—to leave out " shall " and insert " may."

[75

He quoted Mr. Gladstone's undertaking as to the Force in 1886, that they would not be put to prejudice as regarded either term of service or authority. The hardship on the officers was illustrated by the case of a man drawing £255 a year, only getting a pension of £93; £237 producing a pension of £75, and £191 a pension of £48. As regarded men, a man who had joined at 21 and served something like 10 years would be entitled under scale proposed to about 9/- per week.—(P.D., vol. xv., p. 112; T.D., vol. xxv., p. 45.)

A discussion took place as to the precise position in which matters were, which was summed up as follows:

Mr. MATTHEWS:—"The Chief Secretary has stated the intention of the Government to be that the gradual reduction shall not be compulsory on the Lord-Lieutenant."

Mr. MORLEY:—"What I said was that you are not to suppose that each particular withdrawal is to be necessarily within six months accompanied by a corresponding reduction."

Mr. MATTHEWS:—"I quite agree, that is what the Chief Secretary said. The reduction is not to be compulsory on the Lord-Lieutenant in consequence of the withdrawal, but the Lord-Lieutenant is to act as the requirements of the Force in other parts of Ireland make it proper for him to act. The Sixth Schedule more or less roughly indicates that view on the part of the Government. Under these circumstances the word "shall" becomes totally inappropriate."

Mr. GLADSTONE:—"We do not impose upon the Lord-Lieutenant the necessity for reduction."

Mr. MATTHEWS:—"If you do not mean to lay an obligation on him why do you say he "shall" reduce?"—(P.D., vol. xv., p. 25; T.D., vol. xxv., p. 46)

After one and a half hour's discussion,

The Committee divided—
For the Amendment 246
Against the Amendment 278
Majority ... 32
(Division List No. 229.)

Mr. **SEXTON** moved—page 16, line 24— to omit "*local.*"

His argument was that there would be no suitable local authority for some time under which the police force could be placed. Disturbances would occur in Ulster where the local, authority would be in opposition to the Central Legislature.—(P.D., vol. xv., p 130, 5; T.D., vol. xxv., p. 46-7.)

Mr. WYNDHAM quoted Mr. Fowler on 1st June. When he said, "by using the words 'local police force,' it is made impossible to create an armed force;" also Mr. Gladstone and Mr. Morley on same date.—(P.D., vol. xv., p. 136-9; T.D., vol. xxv., p. 47.)

Mr. GLADSTONE opposed Amendment, admitting "that this course involved a narrowing of privileges which under happier circumstances might probably be left unimpaired."—(P.D., vol. xv., p. 142; T.D., vol. xxv., p. 47.)

Mr. JOHN REDMOND spoke in favour of Amendment, as also Mr. DILLON.

Mr. T. W. RUSSELL considered Mr. Sexton had now shown his hand regarding the treatment Ulster would receive from an Irish Parliament.—(P.D., vol. xv., p. 148; T.D., vol. xxv., p. 49.)

Colonel SAUNDERSON quoted Mr. Dillon's cross-examination at Cork, in 1891, when he said he hoped yet to "break up and disorganise" the Royal Irish Constabulary.—(P.D., vol. xv., p. 150; T.D., vol. xxv., p. 49.)

After an hour's discussion,

The Committee divided—

For the Amendment	110
Against the Amendment	237
Majority	127

The Minority was made up of some few Radicals voting with the Irish Party.—(Division List No. 230.)

[77

After some further discussion, at ten o'clock the "Gag" was applied.

On the question "That Clause XXX. as amended stand part of the Bill,"

The Committee divided—

For the Clause	315
Against the Clause	289
Majority ...	26

(Division List No. 232.)

Clause XXX.—No. XXIX. as amended.

[*As Amended in Committee. The italics show the words added. The words in black type bracketed were deleted.*]

(1.) The forces of the Royal Irish Constabulary and Dublin Metropolitan Police shall, when and as local police forces are from time to time established in Ireland in accordance with the [**Sixth**] *Fifth* Schedule to this Act, be gradually reduced and ultimately cease to exist as mentioned in that Schedule ; and *thereupon the Acts relating to such forces shall be repealed, and no forces organized and armed in like manner, or otherwise than according to the accustomed manner of a civil police, shall be created under any Irish Act;* and after the passing of this Act, no officer or man shall be appointed to either of those forces ;

Provided that until the expiration of six years from the appointed day, nothing in this Act shall require the Lord Lieutenant to cause either of the said forces to cease to exist, if as representing Her Majesty the Queen he considers it inexpedient.

(2.) The said two forces shall, while they continue, be subject to the control of the Lord Lieutenant as representing her Majesty, and the members thereof shall continue to receive the same salaries, gratuities, and pensions, and hold their appointments on the same tenure as heretofore, and those salaries, gratuities, and pensions, and all the expenditure incidental to either force, shall be paid out of the Exchequer of the United Kingdom.

(3.) When any existing member of either force retires under the provisions of the [**Sixth**] *Fifth* Schedule to this Act, the Treasury may award to him a gratuity or pension in accordance with that Schedule.

(4.) Those gratuities and pensions and all existing pensions payable in respect of service in either force, shall be paid by the Treasury to the payee out of the Exchequer of the United Kingdom.

(5.) Two-thirds of the net amount payable in pursuance of this section out of the Exchequer of the United Kingdom shall be repaid to that Exchequer from the Irish Exchequer.

CLAUSES XXXI., XXXII., XXXIII., XXXV., XXXVI., XXXVIII., were then added to the Bill without discussion.

(Division Lists Nos. 232-238.)

Clause **XXXIX.** was negatived.

CLAUSES XXXIV., XXXVII., XL., were agreed to. (July 20.)

Financial Clauses.

FOURTH COMPARTMENT.

The debate on these Clauses extended over five sittings, and occupied twenty-seven and a half hours. (July 21, 24, 25, 26, 27.)

On the question that the Clause be read a second time, Mr. CHAMBERLAIN called attention to the following facts—

(1.) This was the Third Financial scheme of the present Bill.

(2.) No single Financial return connected with any of the three schemes was in agreement with others.

(3.) The principal of the 1886 Bill was payment according to taxable capacity—one-quarter of the total contribution of the United Kingdom.

(4.) This was succeeded by a gratuitous gift of, at first £1,400,000, and later on £1,700,000, being balance of duties collected in one but paid on goods consumed in another country.

(5.) By the introduction of this feature, Ireland's taxable contribution was reduced to one-twenty-fifth.

(6.) In February last a new principle was presented, reducing it to one-twenty-sixth.

(7.) Then another present of £500,000 was decided upon, which reduced the quota to one-thirtieth.

So much for previous ideas. As regards the present scheme :—

(a) One-third of the Irish Revenue was to be taken because it was represented as the present payment of Ireland by the Government.

(b) This however, was no criterion of what it might represent six months after the Bill would come into force.

(c) This one-third represented a working out at one-twenty-seventh or one-twenty-eighth.

(d) But the Government stultified all this by deducting from this, one-third of Constabulary cost and the cost of collection of Revenue, with the result that this one-twenty-seventh or one-twenty-eighth resolved itself into one-fortieth.

Therefore it came about that whereas the first representation was that the quota would be one-fifteenth, it really worked out one-twenty-fifth; secondly, the one-twenty-sixth went up to one-thirtieth; and thirdly, the one-twenty-eighth would only give one-fortieth. The similarity of the schemes was that somehow or other the Irish Government was to have a surplus of £500,000.

The objections to Government scheme were of two kinds; the method and the result. Every figure employed was an estimate which varied from day to day. For instance, in the present year Irish Customs are returned at £21,000 less than last year; Excise at £58,000; and Stamps at £48,000.—(P.D., vol. xv., p. 213-7; T.D., vol. xxv., p. 56-7.)

The Right Hon. Gentleman dealt with case of transfer of business, illicit distillation, death duties, and effect of Irish Members in case of Budget, in Imperial Parliament.—(P.D., vol. xv., p. 219-20; T.D., vol. xxv., p. 57-8.)

The three important points of difference between the various schemes of 1886 and 1893 were these :—

> (1.) In 1886, the proposal was to pay one-third of the Constabulary cost, but the savings as the force, gradually reduced, all went to reduce the British contribution till if was wiped out. Now Great Britain only got one-third of the savings.
>
> (2.) Great Britain obtained control over Excise and Customs in 1893, and in case of war Ireland's contribution was fixed at one-twelfth — a manifest improvement on the Bill of 1886, where no such provisions were made. Still the question arose—why, if Ireland was to pay one-twelfth in time of actual war, should she only pay one-fortieth when heavy expense was incurred, year in year out, to prepare for, if not prevent war, with great military expenditure?
>
> (3.) In the early schemes, the cost of collection was tacked on to local expenditure. Now the proposal

was to put it down as Imperial Expenditure. The cost of collecting Irish taxes for Irish purposes was to be a matter of Imperial Expenditure! Why? The Government made a mistake of £350,000 as regards Excise, and so to provide the surplus reduced by this amount the cost of collection had to be transferred.

Coming to deal with the Irish Budget, the Right Hon. Gentleman presented the case as follows:—

> The gross Irish contribution was represented as £2,280,000, or one-twenty-eighth of the Imperial expenditure. Deducting the cost of collection, the nett contribution would be £2,050,000, or one-thirtieth of the nett expenditure, so that the quota was raised artificially by making Ireland the present of cost of collection.
>
> Ireland last year paid £2,103,000, but if £486,000 for Police and £227,000 for Excise collection be taken off, the gross contribution calculated by Government— (£2,280,000)—the nett figure would be £1,560,000, or £543,000 less than Ireland paid last year.—(P.D., vol. xv., p. 225-6: T.D., vol. xxv., p. 59.)
>
> The Treasury Returns were inaccurate, and this difference would probably turn out to be £700,000. In two returns presented on the one day there was a difference of £200,000.
>
> Testing the wealth of Ireland by the death duties calculation, the figure was one-eighteenth, and this he contended was what she *ought* to pay. Judged by this standard, Ireland under the Government proposal would be paying £1,800,000 less than she ought.— (P.D., vol. xv., p. 230; T.D., vol. xxv., p. 60.)

In reply to Mr. Goschen,

Mr. FOWLER, speaking after Mr. Chamberlain, put the

error in calculation down at £350,000.—(P.D., vol. xv., p. 233; T.D., vol. xxv., p. 61.)

Continuing, Mr. FOWLER said the percentage of payment to Imperial Revenue by Ireland was:—

1890	8.03
1891	7.99;
1892 ...	7.90;
1893 ...	7.85;

therefore, Ireland was at the moment contributing one-twelfth. The present Tax Revenue of Ireland was £6,936,000, and the cost of the Government of Ireland, including the deficit on the Post Office, £4,634,000; which left the contribution, exclusive of cost of collection, at £2,302,000. The cost of collection was included in the gross Imperial charge Ireland was credited with—one-third of her Revenue, i.e., Customs, Excise, Stamps, Income Tax, Crown Lands and miscellaneous receipts. These sums gave a total of £4,660,000. This left the contribution to the Imperial Exchequer at £2,262,000, to which should be added a very small amount of taxation collected in England from persons living in Ireland—£14,000. The difference between Mr. Chamberlain and himself was only about £25,000.

Mr. CHAMBERLAIN dissented, and said no reference was made to the Constabulary.

Mr. FOWLER said he was taking the Constabulary at its full charge. Ireland would receive one-third, Great Britain two-thirds of the Revenue collected in Ireland—£8,512,000. The calculated cost of collection was £235,000; the proportionate cost of collection of amount payable as between articles consumed in Ireland and Great Britain being £120,000.

What was done was to take the whole cost of Imperial Expenditure, adding the cost of collecting, making £63,000,000; and to this amount the Irish contribution would represent a proportion of 3·62 per cent., or one-twenty-seventh or one-twenty-eighth. Ireland was given her share of Imperial Receipts, such as profits on Mint, Receipts from Suez Canal Shares, &c. The Police Grant of £500,000 was a distinct bonus to Ireland, justified on politic and financial grounds.—(P.D., vol. xv., p. 232-7; T.D., vol. xxv., p. 61-2.)

Taking the average for five years Ireland had paid something between one-eighteenth and one-twenty-second of the Income Tax and Death Duties.

In reply to Mr. Brodrick Mr. FOWLER said:—"This was not taking the property assessed to be Death Duty, but the Duty paid." Whereupon Mr. Goschen remarked:—"That is no test." —(P.D., vol. xv., p. 239; T.D., vol. xxv., p. 627.)

Taking the whole assessment of Income Tax the contribution of Ireland was one-twenty-second.

Applying the political economists' test—*i.e.* allowing £12 a head, which was not to be taxed at all—to the returns of population made by Mr. Giffen in 1886, the taxable income of Great Britain was shown to be £800,000,000, and that of Ireland £15,000,000.— (P.D., vol. xv., p. 241; T.D., vol. xxv., p. 63.)

Mr. JOHN REDMOND advocated the appointment of a Special Commission on this question, and the giving to the Irish Parliament the collection of all taxes, revenue included. Previous financial returns had been proved to be wrong; what guarantee had they that this was correct?—(P.D., vol. xv., p. 242-53; T.D., vol. xxv., p. 63-4.)

Sir JOHN LUBBOCK pointed out that from Government Returns it appeared that while Ireland's Parliamentary representation was more than 15 per cent. her contribution to expenditure was under eight per cent. Imperial grants had been so large that Ireland's nett contribution was only three per cent. to Great Britain's 97. In grants for Public Works, Scotland had received £9,400,000, and England £50,000,000, while the amounts remitted were—Scotland £365,000; England £474,000, and Ireland £10,400,000. From the official returns it appeared that Ireland would only pay 6s. 6d. per head, while Englishmen and Scotchmen would have to pay 35s. In 1886 Mr. Gladstone had said Irishmen would pay 13s. 5d. to the 30s. paid in Great Britain, and he did not consider it an inequitable arrangement, but now it was a case of 6s. 6d. versus 35s.—(P.D., vol. xv., p. 254-7; T.D., vol. xxv., p. 64-5.)

Mr. COHEN pointed out that not a word had been vouchsafed in explanation of why cost of collection should be borne by England. *Surely reason would suggest that if Ireland was to have two-thirds, she should pay two-thirds of the cost of collection.*—(P.D., vol. xv., p. 331; T.D., vol. xxv., p. 71.)

Mr. G. BALFOUR said the last return of the Government showed that the present net contribution of Ireland to the Imperial expenditure was £2,113,000. To that he added a sum of £225,000, which he understood the right hon. gentleman opposite to say would be the cost of collecting the revenue in Ireland, and thus he arrived at the gross total of Ireland's contribution as £2,338,000. The gross contribution of Ireland as proposed under the scheme was £2,276,000, and subtracting that from the former sum, the loss to the Imperial Exchequer was £62,000. To that was to be added the charge for the constabulary. The right hon. gentleman would say that that was a vanishing charge, but in the first year it would amount to £486,000. These two sums added together gave a total loss to the British Exchequer of £548,000. But that was not all. There was an item in the account of the expenditure of Ireland amounting to £120,000 for public works and buildings, and another item of £152,000 for railways. These two sums added together made £272,000, and therefore he arrived at the conclusion that the total loss under the new system would be £820,000. If they subtracted this sum from £2,276,000 the result was £1,456,000, which represented the true net contribution of Ireland to the Imperial expenditure. That amount was about equivalent to 1-42nd part of the Imperial expenditure. In order to arrive at the net contribution payable by Ireland to this country, the right hon. gentleman on Friday last adopted this method—he took the total revenue of Ireland, and then the amount of the Irish charges, and subtracted the latter from the former. If they compared the contribution of Ireland in 1891-92 with her contribution in 1892-93, a considerable discrepancy would be found. In the former year there was a sum of £250,000 spent on railways, and it was that sum which made the difference. This expenditure on public works was in the nature of a special and exceptional charge, and ought not to enter into the calculation at all. The same remark would apply also to the charge for the Constabulary.—(P.D., vol. xv., p. 338; T.D., vol. xxv., p. 72.)

In the course of further speeches,

Sir WM. HARCOURT referred to "the fallacy that runs through the whole of the fly-sheet which has been distributed by the hon. member for Surrey. Why, the figures are absolutely fallacious from beginning to end. He takes the Prime Minister's figures of 1886 in order to compare them with the present figures, and he deducts the £500,000 from the one and not from the other. A man who makes calculations in that way cannot carry any possible weight in matters of this kind. It is no use arguing on figures of that description."

Mr. BRODRICK: "May I remind the Chancellor of the Exchequer that the Prime Minister himself stated in his speech of 1886 that he confidently expected the charge for the constabulary would not exceed a million."

Sir WM. HARCOURT: "If that were so, I do not see how the Prime Minister could have arrived at the results he stated on that occasion. If the hon. gentleman chooses to rely on figures of that description I cannot help it.—(P.D., vol. xv., p. 344; T.D., vol. xxv., p. 73.)—I have shown how for years you have lost £500,000 in Irish contributions. In 1889-90 the contribution was £2,500,000. Last year it was barely more than £2,000,000. That has gone in endeavouring to buy off the unpopularity of your Coercion Bill. You have had in that time to use more force, and your expenditure on force has been greater than it was before. You have had to offer the Irish bribes as the price of peace."—(P.D., vol. xv., p. 356; T.D., vol. xxv., p. 76.)

Mr. JACKSON considered that the Chancellor of the Exchequer hardly did himself justice, and certainly did not do justice to the leader of the Opposition, when he spoke of the efforts made to relieve pressing and urgent distress in Ireland as a bribe given to buy the hostility of hon. gentlemen below the gangway. At the time that expenditure was undertaken they were threatened with a grave calamity in Ireland.

The CHANCELLOR of the EXCHEQUER: "I did not say he ought not to have done it." (Oh.)

Mr. JACKSON: Then why did the right hon. gentleman condemn the expenditure of these large sums? (An hon. member.—He said they were bribes).—(P.D., p. 358; T.D., p. 75.) The right hon. gentleman had hardly behaved quite fairly or frankly with the members of the Opposition. He spoke over and over again of the year 1892-3, and then he said that he would take three years as establishing what he called the normal condition of the account. It was true, he admitted, that in those years there had been exceptional expenditure; but that very fact destroyed altogether the accuracy of the statement that those three years were to be taken as normal years. From figures which he had himself extracted he found that £240,000 was about the average yearly expenditure in Ireland upon public works and buildings during the 15 years prior to 1890-1. In the three years which the right hon. gentleman had taken as normal, the expenditure under this head jumped up from the figure named to £409,000, £573,000 and £336,000 respectively. These years could not, therefore, be taken as normal. The expenditure which had been incurred on railways in Ireland would result in great advantage to that country, but the method of computation adopted by the right hon. gentleman was practically to capitalize against Great Britain that large expenditure. This was unfair, because it credited Ireland with an exceptional expenditure which would cease.— (P.D., vol. xv., p. 361 ; T.D., vol. xxv., p. 77.)

The fact that the Income Tax upon trades and manufactures did not produce as much in proportion in Ireland as it did in this country was due to the fact that there was a much larger proportion of the population of this country engaged in manufactures than was the case in Ireland. In working out this subject of the Income Tax he had alighted upon the curious fact that whereas in

England the value of land assessed to the Income Tax under Schedule B had fallen between 1880 and 1891 from £51,000,000 to £41,000,000, and in Scotland from £8,770,000 to £6,300,000, in Ireland it had only fallen from £9,980,000 to £9,410,000. That fact showed that there had not been that large diminution of profit from that source in Ireland that there had been in Great Britain, and that the impression that Ireland was worse off now than she was in 1880 was not well-founded. The Post Office Savings Banks' returns showed that the deposits in the Irish Post Office Savings Banks had risen from £1,500,000 in 1880 to £3,900,000 in 1891.—(P.D., vol. xv., p. 366; T.D., vol. xxv., p. 78).

Mr. RENTOUL said:—

" With reference to the relative cost of the police in England Scotland, and Ireland, referred to by the Chancellor of the Exchequer, a pertinent question was—To what part of Ireland was the heavy cost of the police to be attributed ? He found that while there was one policeman for each 635 persons in England, in county Down there was one for every 1,052 persons only, and in Antrim one for every 1,003 persons. It was clear, therefore, that if the police cost 6s. 10d. per head in Ireland, as compared with 2s. 10d. in England, it was not in the Unionist counties, but among the right hon. gentleman's own friends, in the places where the union of hearts throbbed strongest, that the cost of the Irish police was chiefly incurred."—(P.D., vol. xv., p. 380; T.D., vol. xxv., p. 79.)

Mr. GOSCHEN said:—

"I will place what I consider to be the real facts of the case before the Committee in a few sentences. According to the last return which they placed before the Committee, the Government put the Imperial expenditure at £62,900,000. The chief point in dispute with regard to the next figure is as to the cost of collection. The President of the Local Government Board said, 'You must take the exact amount paid in Ireland;' but that which is paid in Ireland is no criterion, because there are many Irish charges which are paid in England. Nor am I prepared to say that you ought to deduct the whole from the Imperial expenditure. You ought to look at the revenue contributed by each of the three parts of the United Kingdom, and then deduct from each of the three the corresponding cost of collection. (Hear, hear.) That is the only business-like way of proceeding." (Cheers.)—(P.D., vol. xv., p. 388; T.D., vol. xxv., p. 80-1.)

"The first balance-sheet showed a surplus of £500,000, but it was found that the excise revenue would give £300,000 less than had been calculated, and it was therefore necessary to revise the estimates—to start a new principle, and to adopt a new canon, that Ireland should pay what it pays now. That was not told us on the first reading. (Cheers.) It was only told us on the second reading of the new clause, which, after we have been over two months in Committee, is now presented to the House. (Cheers.) This £300,000 has to be made up, and the right hon. gentleman said, "We must give them £500,000 for the constabulary; then they will have the surplus that they want." (The Chancellor of the Exchequer:—We always proposed it.) Then, as now, you must have a surplus. The view of hon. members below the gangway is that unless you start them with a good round sum bankruptcy would be possible. You must, therefore, give them £500,000, and the constabulary offer, in the eyes of the Government, the best source of contribution that could be offered."—(P.D., vol. xv., p. 389; T.D., vol. xxv., p. 81.)

"The idea is clearly this, that Ireland cannot do without this contribution. ("No.") Well, can Ireland do without it? I am not sure that Irish members are not perfectly right in maintaining that unless they have this £500,000 they will find great difficulty in making both ends meet. (Hear, hear.) That is a confession— I do not wish to introduce one word to jar on their susceptibilities —but that is a confession that Ireland is too poor. I do not say whether it is correct or incorrect. Well, if Ireland does not contribute the sum which the Government think it ought to contribute to the British Exchequer, then it might be able to stand alone."

Mr. CLANCY: "If you keep your hands out of our pockets we can stand alone. (Cheers.)"

Mr. GOSCHEN: "A charming confession! If we keep our hands out of your pockets then you can manage to run alone. Very well. The Government do not intend to keep their hands out of your pockets. I see a very great danger in that remark, for if the hon. gentleman holds that the Government put their hands too deep into Irishmen's pockets now, what prospect is there of a friendly settlement six years hence?"—(P.D., vol. xv., p. 394-5; T.D., vol. xxv., p. 82.)

"It has been proved that the right hon. gentleman (Mr. Gladstone) does not eliminate that danger (Irish distress), and if the same sort of famine and danger which occurred in 1889 and 1890 were to recur under Home Rule, I do not feel at all certain that Ireland would not be compelled to appeal once more to the British Exchequer, and if such an appeal were made it would be met."—(P.D., vol. xv., p. 398; T.D., vol. xxv., p. 83.)

"Now, the view taken by the members from Ireland is that Ireland is immensely over-taxed at the present time. They hold that that over-taxation dates back to the Union. I have heard the theory put forward that they have been over-taxed in the whole to the extent of £300,000,000 sterling. The first error in that is that when they speak of contribution they never deduct from it any excess contribution made by this country to Ireland. (Cheers.) But what is more important is to consider not only the gross but the net revenue, and hon. members will have to deduct from the enormous sum, which they say Ireland has paid too much, what they have received in excess of the proportion due to them as compared with England and Scotland, and also the amounts collected in Ireland as taxes paid by the English consumer. Is the great-grandson of the British taxpayer of the first part of the century now to repay to the great-grandson of the Irish taxpayer any sum over-paid by Ireland? I think that would be fantastic finance. But see the danger that lurks in the idea. It is this—that from the time of the Union England and Ireland have not been one nation. Let the Committee mark. The statement is, "The Irish contribution at present is no less than 8 per cent.," but we have been elaborately assured tonight by the Chancellor of the Exchequer that Ireland's contribution is to be precisely what she has been paying. My right hon. friend the Prime Minister says, "they have paid 8 per cent., and we propose to fix their contribution at a little over 4 per cent. To continue their present contribution would be a prolongation of injustice." What dangerous language for a Prime Minister to use, to hold that it would be a prolongation of injustice, whereas his own Chancellor of the Exchequer states that the precise contribution is to be prolonged, and to be prolonged because it is at present being paid. (Cheers.) But my right hon. friend says, "I am sorry to say it is an injustice, and its continuance will be an injustice." Dangerous words for a Prime Minister to use. If Ireland pay too much, I ask the attention of the Committee to this point—if they pay too much, Why do they pay too much? When did they begin to pay too much? Under what system of taxation did they pay too much?"

Colonel NOLAN: "When you raised the whisky tax."

Mr. GOSCHEN: "Precisely. When we raised the whisky tax in 1853, and when we extended the income-tax to Ireland for the first time. The first effective step was taken by the Chancellor of the Exchequer in 1853. Who was he? He was the present Prime Minister."

Mr. GLADSTONE: "As my right hon. friend has mentioned that, he ought to have mentioned the enormous pecuniary remission that was made at that time."

Mr. GOSCHEN: "I am going to mention that. What was my right hon. friend's defence of the spirit duties?"

Mr. GLADSTONE: "I made no defence."

Mr. GOSCHEN: "The defence you made in 1853."

Mr. GLADSTONE: "I made no defence."

Mr. GOSCHEN: "Your justification. In 1853 the right hon. gentleman increased the spirit duties. He was violently attacked by the Irish members of that day. One of the Irish members said then that the right hon. gentleman in reply had made one of the jauntiest speeches ever made by a Chancellor of the Exchequer; and it was said that he made sneers and insinuations against the Irish members which they did not deserve." (Laughter.)—(P.D., vol. xv., p. 400-3; T.D., vol. xxv., p. 84-5.)

After ten and a half hours' debate

The Committee divided on the Second Reading of the Clause.

For the Second Reading	226
Against the Second Reading	191
Majority ...	35

(Division List No. 296.) (July 24.)

Mr. J. REDMOND moved the omission of the first sub-section in order to raise a clear issue. Clause X. as it originally stood gave the Irish Legislature control, collection, and management of the taxes in Ireland immediately, with the exception of the customs.

Mr. GLADSTONE said he was not able to assent to the statement that the amendment raised a clear issue. If the amendment was carried the omission of the sub-section would leave things exactly as they were, that was to say, the collection and management of the revenue would be in the hands of the Imperial authorities, and therefore the hon. member would of course require to proceed by further provisions in order to attain his end.—(P.D., vol. xv., p. 492-3; T.D., vol. xxv., p. 94.)

Mr. A. BALFOUR said "the Bill, as he understood it, contemplated that the whole of the Royal Irish Constabulary should be withdrawn as soon as the new Irish Legislature sent a certificate to the Lord-Lieutenant that local police in any county had been provided. It was not, he presumed, intended by the Government to intrust to such local police the whole responsibility of protecting the Imperial revenue, and yet they would apparently deprive themselves, or they might find that they had deprived themselves, by this Bill of the existing machinery for that purpose."

Mr. GLADSTONE quite admitted that the question raised by the right hon. gentleman in respect of the collection of the Imperial revenue by the local police was one which might require some consideration, but it was not an imminent or pressing question at the present time.—(P.D., vol. xv., p. 494-5 ; T.D., vol. xxv., p. 95.)

Col. SAUNDERSON said "if the Prime Minister had looked at the amendment paper he would have seen a later amendment providing that the tribute was to be paid only when the the surplus in the Irish Exchequer was not less than £500,000. This proposal was an old friend. The Irish landlords had been dealt with in the same way. The tenant was told to pay first the shopkeeper, then his dues, then to retain sufficient to enjoy life, and, having fulfilled all those duties, to pay what was left to the landlords, if he wished."—(P.D., vol. xv., p. 497 ; T.D., vol. xxv., p. 96.)

Mr. CLANCY said "if a deficit occurred, the Irish Government would have no power to make it up; for the Minister who proposed a new tax in Ireland during the next 10 or 20 years would be a very bold man."—(P.D., vol. xv., p. 499: T.D., vol. xxv., p. 96.)

Mr. BALFOUR said "his own view was that they were trying an impossible experiment, and for his part he wished to see it tried, if at all, on the smallest scale possible. The scheme was an impossible one, but they were met by these antagonistic impossibilities on every clause of the Bill. They had always got to consider on every proposal of the Government whether the impossibility on the right was or was not worse than the impossibility on the left."—(P.D., vol. xv., p. 507 ; T.D., vol. xxv., p. 97.)

Mr. SEXTON said "he could only countenance the withholding of the power of collecting the taxes from the Irish Legislature as a provisional arrangement. There was, however, some financial gain to the Irish Parliament in allowing the power of collecting the revenue to remain in the Imperial Parliament for six years—again which he estimated at £25,000 a year."—(P.D., vol. xv., p. 508-13; T.D., vol. xxv., p. 97-8.)

Mr. CARSON said "according to the Clause Ireland would continue to pay to the Imperial Parliament taxes which Mr. Gladstone had described as shabby and unjust."—(P.D., vol. xv., p. 527; T.D., vol. xxv., p. 100).

After about five hours' discussion

The Committee divided—

For the Amendment	53
Against the Amendment	249
Majority ...	196

(Division List No. 240.)

Mr. CHAMBERLAIN moved—line 1— to leave out the words:—

"*The transfer hereinafter mentioned*" *in order to insert the words* "*Parliament otherwise determines.*"

He argued that the Bill brought no finality, but left everything open by the adoption of this transitional period; Mr. Gladstone had spoken of this Bill bringing about a permanent and continuous settlement.

Mr. GLADSTONE: "A continuing settlement."

Mr. CHAMBERLAIN asked whether hon. members saw any difference.—(P.D., vol. xv., p. 535-7; T.D., vol. xxv., p. 101-2).

Mr. GLADSTONE in reply, spoke of "the Devil's advocate." What were the questions not settled? He granted there was the Land Question.

Mr. CHAMBERLAIN: "An obligation of honour."

Mr. GLADSTONE: "Yes, an obligation of honour with respect to facts and circumstances that were then existing, and expressly stated by him, as his right hon. friend must know to be an obligation to these temporary facts and circumstances."—(P.D., vol. xv., p. 539; T.D., vol. xxv., p. 103.)

"Now, what was settled by the Bill? It was settled by the Bill that Ireland should make her own laws. It was settled that Ireland should have two Chambers of Legislature. He wanted to know whether fixing the legislative body was or was not a capital and fundamental portion of any scheme of government for Ireland. They had settled the Executive, the relations between the Executive and the legislative body. (Voices—The Gag.) They had absolutely settled the judiciary. ("Oh.") (Lord R. Churchill.—"All by the closure.") The police had been absolutely fixed. In naming these branches had he not named all the most important branches of a scheme for the government of Ireland with the exception of finance? And with respect to that exception, his right hon. friend had himself said that the most important parts were fixed. In this instance his right hon. friend exhibited, as he did in others, his practice of gross, habitual, and enormous exaggeration." —(P.D., vol. xv., p. 540; T.D., vol. xxv., p. 103.)

Mr. A. BALFOUR having dealt with the settlement of matters by the "gag," said, "there remained the vital question of the Irish members in this House. Was that settled? He appealed to the Government themselves on that point. Clause IX., dealing with them, began with the words 'unless and until Parliament otherwise determines.' The Prime Minister himself had said, when similar words were proffered as an amendment to another clause by the right hon. member for West Birmingham, that their insertion would be a conclusive proof that the clause was a temporary and short-lived one."

Mr. GLADSTONE explained that the words referred to were introduced to show that the 9th Clause was no part of the honourable compact between Great Britain and Ireland.

Mr. BALFOUR said that the meaning of the words of an Act did not depend upon the intention of those who inserted them, but on the words themselves.—(P.D., vol. xv., p. 547; T.D., vol. xxv., p. 105.)

Mr. CHAMBERLAIN said he did not know whether hon. members opposite had refused just now to make themselves parties to the statement of his right hon. friend because they knew what it would involve, but if he himself were guilty of gross, habitual and enormous exaggeration, what was to be said of the hon. member for North Kerry? That hon. member said in the debate on Clause IX.:—"The whole Bill, in fact, had been made transitional and almost experimental in its character, by reason of the provisions deferring the power of the Irish Government for a given period of years in regard to judicial appointments, the land question, and certain financial topics, and therefore it would be in accord with the general character of the Bill that the words should be allowed to stand "—that was to say the question of the retention of the Irish members should be made transitional also. What the hon. member for North Kerry said, and what he himself said, was, that all these points which were questioned in the country and upon which the Unionists had vainly endeavoured to get any information from the Government beforehand had been left in a transitional condition. To them might be added also the question of the police, for the whole position of that force was to be altered after the period of six years.—(P.D., vol. xv., p. 561; T.D., vol. xxv., p. 108.)

There was no reply to Mr. Chamberlain, and after Sir John Lubbock had spoken, although Mr. A. Balfour rose, Mr. Morley moved the closure. There was some excitement occasioned by this, and Mr. Morley said he had not seen the right hon. gentleman rise.

Mr. A. BALFOUR and Mr. FOWLER having spoken,

Mr. GOSCHEN elicited from Mr. Fowler the statement that the question of how much Ireland should pay to Imperial Expenditure ought not to be delegated to a commission.—(P.D., vol. xv., p. 569; T.D., vol. xxv., p. 110.)

After some three hours' discussion.

The Committee divided—

For the Amendment	166
Against the Amendment	226
Majority ...	60

(Division List No. 241.)

Sir JOHN LUBBOCK moved to omit sub-sections 2, 3, 4 and 5.

He pointed out that, as regards Irish complaints, there were poor in England as well as in Ireland. Official returns showed that in case of both Tobacco and Tea, the consumption in Ireland was quite equal to that in Great Britain as a matter of average. Then as regards police Ireland, with a population of 4,700,000, had a charge of £1,500,000; London with 5,000.000 people had a charge of £1,811,000. As regarded Education in England last year over £2,000,000 were raised from local sources without counting school-pence, which amounted to £2,000,000 more; whereby in Ireland the whole expense was borne by the Imperial Exchequer.

On the whole the expense of Government was by no means great as compared with other countries. The revenue raised in Ireland with a population of 4.700,000 was given in Parliamentary Return 334 of the present Session at £7,360,000. Now, if they looked at other countries that was by no means a heavy amount. Holland, with a smaller population, 4,500,000, paid over

£10,000,000; Belgium, with a population of 6,000,000, paid £12,000,000. Under this Bill Ireland was to contribute £1,550,000 for the service of debt, for military and naval expenditure, for diplomatic, and all other joint expenditure. Holland, for military expenditure alone, paid £3,000,000, and Belgium £2,000,000. The revenue raised in Ireland was given in the last return (July 14) at £7,400,000, or £1 7s. 6d. per head. Now the annual expenditure of Belgium was £2 5s., of Holland £2 10s., of France £3 5s. 6d., of Italy £2 1s., of Denmark £2 2s., of Spain £1 18s., of Greece £1 16s., of Hungary £1 19s., and of the United States £2 7s. Even in their own case—the case of Great Britain, which he wondered did not occur to the right hon. gentleman—it was £2 10s. (Hear, hear.) Nobody who looked at the figures could doubt for a moment that, if during the last century Ireland had been an independent country, her taxation would have been far heavier than had been the case.—(P.D., vol. xv., p. 573–4; T.D., vol. xxv., p. 111.)

Mr. BRODRICK, dealing with question of Excise, said: "The Government proposal meant that Irishmen who all round paid 13s. per head to Excise should pay 2s. 7d. to Imperial charges, while Englishmen who paid 15s. to Excise should pay 10s. to Imperial charges. In Denmark every man contributed 6s. 1d. towards the national defences; in Switzerland every man paid 8s. 9d. towards those defences; but under the proposal of the Government every man in Ireland would only pay 3s. 6d., while in Great Britain every man would pay 19s. 9d. Under these circumstances he thought that to give this surplus of £500,000 to Ireland without retaining any hold over the Irish expenditure was a gross injustice to the working men of this country."—(P.D., vol. xv., p. 581; T.D., vol. xxv., p. 112.)

Col. NOLAN contended that dividing the amount by population Ireland paid 10s. per head instead of 3s. 6d.—(P.D., vol. xv., p. 583; T.D., vol. xxv., p. 112.)

Sir RICHARD TEMPLE said:—"The position of Ireland differed from smaller European powers because not one was secure against invasion by a great power, whereas Ireland was defended. All other nations had to pay one-half of their taxation away for defence and national obligations, but here England had to pay two-thirds."—(P.D., vol. xv., p. 586: T.D., vol. xxv., p. 113.)

After two and a half hours' debate

The Committee divided—

For the Amendment	...	...	205
Against the Amendment	...	...	252
		Majority ...	47

(Division List No. 242.)

A discussion took place with regard to composition and scope of Committee to decide on matters of General Revenue in future, as between Ireland and Great Britain under Bill.—(P.D., vol. xv., p. 671-85; T.D., vol. xxv.. p. 123.)

Mr. CLANCY moved to add to the beginning of the fourth sub-section the words:—

" *Whenever the surplus available for the Irish Government amounts to not less than £500,000.*"

He explained that his object was to guarantee a surplus to the Irish Government of £500,000. It was said that this was a part of the doctrines of the Land League, but this would not be the first time during the past ten or twelve years that Parliament had been engaged in passing into law the programme of the original Land League. The mistakes which had already been made as to the financial scheme under Home Rule led him to be suspicious of all returns, and he would be slow to embark on the task of working a scheme of self-government without being certain whether he would have a surplus or a deficit in the first year of administration.—(P.D., vol. xv., p. 685; T.D.. vol. xxv., p. 126.)

Mr. GLADSTONE said:—"Upon the paper, according to the estimates that had been framed, the Government showed a surplus of £500,000, which, if the estimates were realized, would be to the credit of Ireland when she took her portion. That was the whole meaning of the surplus. There was no such thing as a surplus earmarked, and there was no such thing legally as a surplus of £500,000. As he understood it, the real meaning and aim of this Amendment was that, whenever in the balance-sheet of Ireland between revenue and expenditure there was a surplus of less than £500,000, then the Imperial contribution was to be reduced by one-fourth. (A Voice:—No; it was to be reduced to nothing.) Perhaps the hon. member would kindly explain."

Mr. J. REDMOND explained that, supposing in some years the surplus of Ireland should be £490,000 instead of £500,000, the effect of the amendment in that case would be that the Imperial contribution of Ireland would be diminished by £5,000.

Mr. GLADSTONE replied that his objection remained in full. —(P.D., vol. xv., p. 693; T.D., vol. xxv., p. 125.)

Mr. COLLINGS said:—"The member for North Dublin had said that by the Act of Union the Irish people were robbed; but, whether that were so or not, it was abundantly clear that by this Bill the people of Great Britain were to be robbed. The hon. member challenged the statement that a burden would be imposed upon the British taxpayer. That, however, was the fact; and every hon. member for Great Britain would be able to go to his constituency and tell them that the cost of the present proposal to them would be £4,000 a year. That was the average for each constituency. For the City of Birmingham, however, the cost would be £32,000 a year, which was equivalent to a 4d. rate. That city would have to pay £32,000 as its contribution towards carrying out the scheme of the Government."—(P.D., vol. xv., p. 700; T.D., vol. xxv., p. 127.)

Mr. SEXTON denied this, and dealt with all the figures in detail.—(P.D., vol. xv., p. 707-17; T.D., vol. xxv., p. 128.)

Mr. CHAMBERLAIN, in a final speech, said that their contention was that Ireland was being asked to pay £1,800,000 less than she ought, and on that issue they intended to go to their constituents. Interrupted by Mr. Roby with the remark, "Under the circumstances" apropos of the Bill being regarded as satisfactory by the Ministerialists, the right hon. gentleman punctuated each sentence afterwards with the quotation. The reference to "Herod" and cries of "Judas" were succeeded by the scene of riot which is now a matter of history.

At ten o'clock the "Gag" was applied,

The Committee divided—

For the First Financial Clause	321
Against the First Financial Clause	288
Majority ...	33

(Division List No. 244)

Another division was taken on the next Clause, the remainder being "agreed to."

The postponed Clauses, xiv., xv., xvi. were then added to the Bill without discussion, as also the entire Schedules with the exception of No. 5 and the Preamble.—(P.D., vol. xv., p. 734-5; T.D. vol. xxv., p. 134; Division Lists No. 245-251.)—(July 27th.)

THE DIVISIONS ON THE HOME RULE BILL.

BRITISH MAJORITIES AGAINST MR. GLADSTONE'S SCHEME.

Division.	Government Vote.			Opposition Vote.			British majority against Government.
	British.	Irish.	Total.	British.	Irish.	Total.	
April 21.—Second reading. Sir M. H. Beach's amendment	268	79	347	282	22	304	14
May 8.—Committee. Closure	171	72	243	175	20	195	4
May 8.—Committee. To report progress	233	74	307	244	21	265	11
May 8.—Committee. That Chairman leave chair	231	73	304	235	22	257	4
May 9.—Clause 1. Mr. Bartley's amendment	217	75	292	235	22	257	18
May 10.—Clause 1. Mr. T. W. Russell's amendment	221	74	295	228	16	244	7
May 11.—Clause 1. To report progress, &c.	230	74	304	239	21	260	9
May 12.—Clause 1. Closure	232	76	308	241	19	260	9
May 12.—Clause 1. That Clause 1 stand part of Bill	235	74	309	246	21	267	11
May 15.—Clause 2. Mr. Cavendish's amendment, Clause 2	203	72	275	208	20	228	5
May 15.—Clause 2. Mr. A. Cross's amendment	223	73	296	229	22	251	6
May 16.—Clause 2. Mr. G. Lawson's amendment	193	72	265	195	20	215	2
May 30.—Amendment. That Clause 3 be postponed	205	68	273	222	18	240	17
May 30.—Clause 3. Viscount Wolmer's amendment	190	69	259	219	19	238	29
May 31.—Clause 3. General Goldsworthy's amendment	196	69	265	202	17	219	6
May 31.—Clause 3. Sir A. Scoble's amendment	206	70	276	218	19	237	12
May 31.— Clause 3. Mr. P. Smith's amendment	207	71	278	216	18	234	9
June 2.—Clause 3. Mr. Byrne's amendment	213	70	283	226	19	245	13
June 2.—Clause 3. Lieut.-Col. Lockwood's amendment	220	74	294	234	20	254	14
June 2.—Clause 3. Mr. W. Brodrick's amendment	215	74	289	230	19	249	15
June 5.—Clause 3. Admiral Field's amendment	223	74	297	238	22	260	15
June 5.—Clause 3. Closure	176	76	252	197	20	217	21

BRITISH MAJORITIES AGAINST MR. GLADSTONE'S SCHEME.—*Continued.*

DIVISION.	Government Vote.			Opposition Vote.			British majority against Government.
	British.	Irish.	Total.	British.	Irish.	Total.	
June 5.—Clause 3. Mr. Tomlinson's amendment	175	76	251	194	20	214	19
June 5.—Clause 3. Mr. G. Balfour's amendment	218	73	291	233	22	255	15
June 6.—Clause 3. Closure ...	233	73	306	253	21	274	20
June 6.—Clause 3. Mr. Butcher's amendment	242	75	317	255	21	276	13
June 6.—Clause 3. Sir H. James's amendment	229	75	304	233	22	255	4
June 6.—Clause 3. Mr. S. Wortley's amendment	166	76	242	171	21	192	5
June 6.—Clause 3. Mr. D. Barton's amendment	217	76	293	230	23	253	13
June 6.—Clause 3. Mr. Carson's amendment	206	76	282	224	22	246	18
June 7.—Clause 3. Mr. J. G. Lawson's amendment	215	73	288	220	22	242	5
June 7.—Clause 3. Closure ...	224	69	293	235	21	256	11
June 8.—Clause 3. Closure ...	213	75	288	235	21	256	22
June 8.—Clause 3. Mr. Bartley's amendment	214	74	288	232	20	252	18
June 8.—Clause 3. Closure ...	157	75	232	170	17	187	13
June 8.—Clause 3. Sir T. Lea's amendment	186	73	259	198	16	214	12
June 9.—Clause 3. Mr. Whiteley's amendment	223	75	298	246	22	268	23
June 12.—Clause 3. Sir J. Lubbock's amendment	211	72	283	234	20	254	23
June 12.—Clause 3. Mr. P. Smith's amendment	189	70	259	203	20	223	14
June 12.—Clause 3. Sir F. Powell's amendment	200	70	270	216	20	236	16
June 12.—Clause 3. Mr. G. Balfour's amendment	193	71	264	211	20	231	18
June 12.—Clause 3. Mr. H. Foster's amendment	179	69	248	192	19	211	13
June 13.—Clause 4. Mr. H. Foster's amendment	200	69	269	215	19	234	15
June 13.—Clause 4. Sir H. James's amendment	116	71	187	127	16	143	11
June 13.—Clause 4. Mr. Boscawen's amendment	198	71	269	214	19	233	16
June 14.—Clause 4. Mr. Rentoul's amendment	193	73	266	209	19	228	16
June 14.—Clause 4. Mr. G. Balfour's amendment	193	73	266	212	19	231	19
June 14.—Clause 4. Mr. G. Balfour's 2nd amendment ...	207	74	281	220	19	239	13
June 14.—Clause 4. Closure ...	206	74	280	223	18	241	17
June 15.—Clause 4. Closure ...	194	74	268	217	18	235	23
June 15.—Clause 4. Mr. Mowbray's amendment	176	73	249	191	17	208	15

BRITISH MAJORITIES AGAINST MR. GLADSTONE'S SCHEME.—*Continued*.

DIVISION.	Government Vote.			Opposition Vote.			British majority against Government.
	British.	Irish.	Total.	British.	Irish.	Total.	
June 15.—Clause 4. Mr. Wyndham's amendment	190	73	263	211	20	231	21
June 16.—Clause 4. Major Darwin's amendment	187	71	258	200	20	220	13
June 16.—Clause 4. Mr. H. Plunkett's amendment	184	69	253	191	20	211	7
June 19.—Clause 4. Mr. Bolton's amendment	214	70	284	230	20	250	16
June 19.—Clause 4. Mr. H. Hobhouse's amendment	221	69	290	237	21	258	16
June 19.—Clause 4. Mr. Carson's amendment	133	68	201	147	17	164	14
June 19.—Clause 4. Mr. Rentoul's amendment	201	69	270	221	20	241	20
June 20.—Clause 4. Viscount Wolmer's amendment	198	72	270	221	19	240	23
June 20.—Clause 4. Viscount Wolmer's amendment	188	72	260	204	19	223	16
June 20.—Clause 4. Closure	199	73	272	218	19	237	19
June 20.—Clause 4. Mr. Brodrick's amendment	198	72	270	219	19	238	21
June 21.—Clause 4. Mr. D. Plunket's amendment	211	73	284	221	21	242	10
June 21.—Clause 4. Mr. Rentoul's amendment	206	73	279	218	20	238	12
June 22.—Clause 4. Mr. Wolff's amendment	230	72	302	235	19	254	5
June 22.—Clause 4. Mr. D. Plunket's amendment	234	73	307	241	20	261	7
June 22.—Clause 4. Mr. Cochrane's amendment	189	71	260	199	19	218	10
June 22.—Clause 4. Closure	207	70	277	223	20	243	16
June 22.—Clause 4. Mr. Cochrane's amendment	206	72	278	223	20	243	17
June 23.—Clause 4. Mr. P. Smith's amendment	201	71	272	212	18	230	11
June 28.—Clause 5. Mr. Hanbury's amendment	197	63	260	210	21	231	13
June 28.—Clause 5. Mr. Hanbury's 2nd amendment	212	68	280	228	21	249	16
June 29.—Mr. Gladstone's Suspension of 12 o'clock Rule	230	72	302	250	21	271	20
June 29.—Mr. Gladstone's Closure Proposal. Mr. Chaplain's motion	236	72	308	258	21	279	22
June 29.—Mr. Gladstone's Closure Proposal. Mr. Russell's amendment	233	73	306	259	20	279	26
June 29.—Mr. Gladstone's Closure Proposal. Baron Rothschild's motion	211	72	283	236	21	257	25

[105

BRITISH MAJORITIES AGAINST MR. GLADSTONE'S SCHEME.—*Continued.*

DIVISION.	Government Vote.			Opposition Vote.			British majority against Government.
	British.	Irish.	Total.	British.	Irish.	Total.	
June 29.—Mr. Gladstone's Closure Proposal. Lord Cranborne's motion	197	73	270	221	21	242	24
June 30.—Mr. Gladstone's Closure Proposal. Mr. Byrne's amendment	204	64	268	223	20	243	19
June 30.—Mr. Gladstone's Closure Proposal. Lord Wolmer's amendment	230	72	302	248	20	268	18
June 30.—Mr. Gladstone's Closure Proposal. Mr. Hayes Fisher's amendment	227	71	298	244	20	264	17
June 30.—Mr. Gladstone's Closure Proposal. Mr. Curzon's amendment	228	72	300	246	20	266	18
June 30.—Mr. Gladstone's Closure Proposal. Main question ...	228	71	299	247	20	267	19
July 3.—Clause 5. Lord Wolmer's amendment	157	73	230	176	20	196	19
July 3.—Clause 5. Mr. Brodrick's amendment	201	73	274	226	21	247	25
July 4.—Clause 5. Mr. Arnold-Forster's amendment	218	75	293	235	21	256	17
July 4.—Clause 5. Mr. Fisher's amendment	208	75	283	227	21	248	19
July 4.—Clause 5. Sir H. James's amendment	114	73	187	122	20	142	8
July 4.—Clause 5. Captain Naylor-Leyland's amendment	140	75	215	147	20	167	7
July 4.—Clause 5. Sir H. James's 2nd amendment	190	72	262	209	20	229	19
July 5.—Clause 5. Mr. T. H. Bolton's amendment	199	75	274	213	16	229	14
July 5.—Clause 5. Closure	185	76	261	202	17	219	17
July 6.—Clause 5. Lord Wolmer's amendment	213	77	290	227	21	248	14
July 6.—Clause 5. Lord Cranborne's amendment	154	77	231	167	18	185	13
July 6.—Clause 5. The Procedure Closure	250	74	324	264	22	286	14
July 6.—Clause 5 as amended be part of Bill	249	75	324	268	21	289	19
July 6.—Clause 6 stand part of Bill	239	76	315	278	22	300	39
July 6.—Clause 7 stand part of Bill	249	76	325	267	22	289	18
July 6.—Clause 8 stand part of Bill	247	76	323	269	22	291	22
July 10.—Clause 9. Mr. Redmond's amendment	213	67	280	244	22	266	31
July 10.—Clause 9. Closure ...	168	73	241	194	17	211	26
July 10.—Clause 9. Mr. Heneage's amendment	166	74	240	193	16	209	27
July 11.—Clause 9. Sir C. Dilke's amendment	140	72	212	168	14	182	28

BRITISH MAJORITIES AGAINST MR. GLADSTONE'S SCHEME.—*Continued.*

DIVISION.	Government Vote.			Opposition Vote.			British majority against Government.
	British.	Irish.	Total.	British.	Irish.	Total.	
July 11.—Clause 9. Mr. Seton-Karr's amendment	180	71	251	202	16	218	22
July 11.—Clause 9. Mr. Rentoul's amendment	184	71	255	211	15	226	27
July 12.—Clause 9. Mr. P. Smith's amendment	210	70	280	230	18	248	20
July 13.—Clause 9. Mr. Gladstone's amendment	247	78	325	280	18	298	33
July 13.—Clause 9 stand part of Bill	249	77	326	281	16	297	32
July 13.—Clause 18 stand part of Bill	250	78	328	276	18	294	26
July 13.—Clause 19 stand part of Bill	247	78	325	273	18	291	26
July 13.—Clause 22 stand part of Bill	241	78	319	268	18	286	27
July 13.—Clause 23 stand part of Bill	236	78	314	262	18	280	26
July 13.—Clause 24 stand part of Bill	223	77	300	247	18	265	24
July 13.—Clause 25 stand part of Bill	213	77	290	244	18	262	31
July 13.—Clause 26 stand part of Bill	214	76	290	239	17	256	25
July 17.—Clause 27. Mr. Morley's amendment	126	68	194	128	14	142	2
July 17.—Clause 27. Mr. Seton-Karr's amendment	174	72	246	186	15	201	12
July 18.—Clause 27. Mr. Balfour's amendment	170	71	241	184	15	199	14
July 20.—Clause 30. Mr. T. H. Bolton's amendment	206	72	278	229	17	246	23
July 20.—Clause 30 stand part of Bill	246	69	315	270	19	289	24
July 20.—Clause 31 stand part of Bill	247	74	321	268	19	287	21
July 20.—Clause 32 stand part of Bill	239	76	315	262	19	281	23
July 20.—Clause 33 stand part of Bill	239	75	314	261	18	279	22
July 20.—Clause 36 stand part of Bill	225	77	302	249	19	268	24
July 20.—Clause 38 stand part of Bill	219	76	295	242	19	261	23
July 24.—Second Reading of Mr. Gladstone's Financial Clauses. First Clause	153	73	226	177	14	191	24
July 26.—To leave out Sub-sections 2, 3, 4, 5, Sir J. Lubbock	179	73	252	187	18	205	8
July 27.—Financial Clause as amended stand part of Bill	243	69	312	270	21	291	27

[107]

BRITISH MAJORITIES AGAINST MR. GLADSTONE'S SCHEME—*Continued*.

DIVISION.	Government Vote.			Opposition Vote.			British majority against Government.
	British.	Irish.	Total.	British	Irish.	Total.	
July 27.—Clause as to Irish Consolidated Fund to be added to Bill	244	77	321	268	20	288	24
July 27.—Postponed Clause 15 be part of Bill	249	77	316	262	21	283	13
July 27.—Postponed Clause 16 be part of Bill	236	77	313	260	20	280	24
July 27.—Schedule 1 be part of Bill	233	77	310	256	21	277	23
July 27.—Schedule 2 be part of Bill	222	68	290	251	22	273	29
July 27.—Schedule 7 be part of Bill	222	77	299	248	20	268	26
July 27.—New schedule be part of Bill	217	76	293	242	21	263	25
July 27.—Preamble to be part of Bill	215	76	291	240	21	261	25

INDEX.

	PAGE
Amendment to Clause I.—defeated (p. 1, l. 11), by Mr. Darling	2
Amendment to Clause I.—defeated (p. 1, l. 11), by Mr. Bartley	2
Amendment to Clause I.—defeated, by Mr. W. Redmond	3
Amendment to Clause I.—assented (p. 1, l. 12), by T. W. Russell	4
Amendment to Clause II.—defeated, by Mr. V. Cavendish	8
Amendment to Clause II.—withdrawn, by Mr. Bartley	9
Amendment to Clause II.—defeated, by Captain Bethell	9
Amendment to Clause II.—defeated, by Mr. A. Cross	9
Amendment to Clause II.—defeated, by Mr. Brodrick	10
Amendment to Clause II.—agreed to, by Sir Henry James	11
Amendment to Clause II.—withdrawn, by Sir Henry James	11
Amendment to Clause II.—defeated, by Mr. Hanbury	12
Amendment to Clause III.—defeated (p. 1, l. 19), by Lord Wolmer	15
Amendment to Clause III.—negatived (p. 1, l. 19), by Lord Wolmer	17
Amendments, series of, to Clause III.—defeated	17
Amendments, series of, to Clause III.—defeated (p. 2, l. 1), by Mr. Bryne	18
Amendments, series of, to Clause III.—defeated (p. 2, l. 1), by Mr. Bartley	17
Amendment to Clause III.—defeated (p. 2, l. 5), by Mr. G. Balfour	18
Amendment to Clause III.—defeated (p. 2, l. 6), by Mr. Butcher	19
Amendment to Clause III.—defeated, "Sedition" after "Treason felony," by Sir Henry James	19
Amendments to Clause III.—defeated, "Criminal conspiracy" and "Explosives," by Mr. Stuart Wortley	20
Amendment to Clause III.—defeated (p. 2, l. 6), by Mr. Barton for Mr. Carson	20
Amendment to Clause III.—assented to (p. 2, l. 6), by Mr. Brodrick	21
Amendment to Clause III.—defeated (p. 2, l. 7), by Mr. Bartley	21
Amendments, series of, to Clause III.—defeated (p. 2, l. 12), by Mr. Whiteley	22
Amendments, series of, to Clause III.—defeated (p. 2, l. 13), by Sir John Lubbock	23
Amendment to Clause III.—defeated (p. 2, l. 16), by Sir F. S. Powell	23
Amendment to Clause IV.—defeated (p. 2, l. 23), by Mr. Griffith Boscawen	27
Amendment to Clause IV.—withdrawn (p. 2, after l. 26), by Mr. Vicary Gibbs	28
Amendment to Clause IV.—defeated (p. 2, l. 30), by Mr. Mowbray	28
Amendment to Clause IV.—withdrawn (p. 2, l. 31), by Mr. Seton-Karr	29
Amendment to Clause IV.—(p. 2, l. 31), by Mr. Gerald Balfour	30
Amendment to Clause IV.—by Mr. Sexton	30
Amendment to Clause IV. (of Mr. G. Balfour), amended	30
Amendment to Clause IV.—defeated (p. 2, l. 1), by Mr. H. Plunkett	31
Amendment to Clause IV.—defeated (p. 2, l. 33), by Mr. T. H. Bolton	32
Amendment to Clause IV.—defeated (p. 2, l. 33), by Mr. Rentoul	32

THE BILL IN COMMITTEE.—INDEX.

	PAGE
Amendment to Clause IV.—defeated (p. 2, l. 33), by Lord Wolmer	33
Amendment to Clause IV.—defeated (p. 2, l. 33), by Lord Wolmer	34
Amendment to the Amendment of Lord Wolmer—defeated, by Mr. Rathbone	34
Amendment to Clause IV. (p. 2, l. 33), after word "or" to insert "(6) whereby any, &c.," by Mr. Parker Smith (negatived without Division)	35
Amendment by Mr. Arnold Forster dealing with prerogative of Mercy	48
Amendment to Clause IV.—defeated (p. 2, l. 33), by Mr. D. Plunket	36
Amendment to Clause IV.—defeated (p. 2, l. 39), by Mr. D. Plunket	37
Amendment to Clause IV.—defeated (p. 2, l. 41), by Mr. Cochrane	38
Amendment to Clause IV.—defeated (p. 2, l. 4), by Mr. Cochrane, on behalf of Lord Randolph Churchill	39
Amendment to Clause IV.—defeated (p. 2, l. 41), by Mr. Parker Smith	40
Amendment to Clause V.—defeated (p. 3, l. 6), by Mr. Hayes Fisher	43
Amendment to Clause V.—defeated (p. 3, l. 6), by Mr. Hanbury	44
Amendment to Clause V.—defeated (p. 3, l. 10), by Lord Wolmer	45
Amendment to Clause V.—defeated (p. 3, l. 10), by Mr. Brodrick	46
Amendment to Clause V.—withdrawn, by Marquis of Carmarthen	48
Amendment to Clause V., by Lord Wolmer	48
Amendments, several, to Clause V.—rejected	48
Amendment to Clause IX.—defeated, by Mr. John Redmond, to leave out sub-section (1)	52
Amendment to Clause IX.—defeated, by Mr. Heneage	52
Amendment to Clause IX.—negatived, by Sir John Lubbock	53
Amendment to Clause IX.—defeated, by Sir Charles Dilke	54
Amendment to omit Sections (3) and (4)—carried, by Mr. Gladstone	55
Amendment to Clause XXVII.—withdrawn (p. 15, l. 21), by Mr. Sexton	59
Amendment to Clause XXVII., by Mr. Morley	60
Amendment to Clause XXVII.—carried, by Mr. Sexton (amendment of Mr. Morley's Amendment)	61
Amendment to Clause XXVII., by Mr. T. W. Russell	62
Amendment to Clause XXVII.—defeated, by Mr. Seton-Karr	62
Amendment to Clause XXX.—defeated, by Mr. Bolton	71
Amendment to Clause XXX., by Mr. Sexton, to omit "local" (p. 16, l. 24)	73
Amendment to Financial Clause by Mr. Redmond (omission of first sub-section), defeated	88
Amendment to Financial Clause by Mr. Chamberlain, defeated	90
Amendment to Financial Clause by Sir J. Lubbock (to omit sub-sections 2, 3, 4 and 5) defeated	93
Amendment to Financial Clause by Mr. Clancy	95
Amendment of Mr. Mowbray to Clause IV., it was pointed out that words of Amendment were left out while context taken from American Constitution	28
Attorney-General in reply to Lord Wolmer	28
Attorney-General in reply to Mr. Chamberlain (as to Sub-section V.)	29
Attorney-General explains powers of Irish Government on Mr. Seton-Karr's Amendment	29
Attorney-General's opinion quoted by Mr. G. Balfour re his Amendment to Clause IV.	30
Attorney-General on Mr. Bolton's Amendment	32
Attorney-General comments on Mr. Rentoul's Amendment "As to fears respecting Ulster, &c."	32

THE BILL IN COMMITTEE.—INDEX.

	PAGE
American Laws of Diversified Character in re "Marriage and Divorce," Mr. Gladstone speaking in opposition to Sir F. S. Powell's Amendment to Clause III.	23
Attack on Government, Bitter, by Mr. Clancy and Mr. Sexton	30
American Constitution, in speaking on his Amendment Lord Wolmer pointed out the words "of an *ex facto* character" as existing in such Constitution	33
American Constitution, quoted by Lord Wolmer, to show words of his Amendment was taken from it	34
Attorney-General in reply to Mr. Rathbone and Mr. Balfour	34 & 35
Attorney-General admitted alteration needed to Sub-section 4	37
Attorney-General thought the Prime Minister must have been misunderstood (in reply to Mr. Plunkett)	37
Ambrose, Mr., said to pass sub-section as it stood suicidal to British Supremacy	48
Acts of 1791 and 1783, quoted by Sir John Gorst in debate on Motion "that Clause I., &c."	6
Ashmead Bartlett, Sir, on Motion "That Clause II., &c.," drew Statement from Mr. Gladstone that the concession regarding Imperial Supremacy was made on Second Reading	13
Byrne, Mr., Amendment to Clause III., "Carrying or using arms, &c."	18
Balfour, Mr. Gerald, Amendment to Clause IV. (p. 2, l. 31), after "law" to insert "in accordance with, &c."	30
Balfour, Mr. Gerald, quotes opinions by Attorney-General and Solicitor-General	30
Brodrick, Mr., reminds Chancellor of Exchequer that Prime Minister in speech of 1886 expected Constabulary charge would not exceed a million	82
Brodrick, Mr., deals with question of Excise	94
Balfour, Mr., points out Mr. Morley and Mr. Bryce at a variance	47
Balfour, Mr., quotes Mr. Morley at Newcastle in 1886, on "the arbitrators and masters of English policy, &c."	53
Balfour, Mr., speaks on Mr. Gladstone's Amendment to Clause IX., and receives heated reply from Mr. Gladstone	56
Balfour, Mr., suggests reserving discussion on general retirement until Clause XXVIII.	63
Balfour, Mr., deals with possibilities of change and the attitude of Irish Members towards Civil Service	65
Balfour, Mr., stated Government Return showed present net contribution of Ireland to Imperial expenditure was £2,113,000	81
Balfour, Mr., spoke as to the withdrawal of Royal Irish Constabulary	88
Balfour, Mr., speaks of the Scheme being impossible	89
Balfour, Mr., deals with settlement of matters by "Gag," and asks as to question of Irish Members in this House	91
"Bill does not create Executive Powers." Mr. Gladstone so states to Mr. Balfour in conversation re Mr. Brodrick's Amendment	10
"Bill discussed under the 'dangerous conditions' outlined by the Prime Minister in 1885" in speech of Sir E. Reed on Mr. Brodrick's Amendment	10
"Bounties." Mr. Bartley's Amendment to Clause III.	21
"Banks, Bills of Exchange" Amendment to Clause III., by Sir John Lubbock	23
Bolton, Mr., supports his Amendment to Clause XXX. by pointing out possible injustice as Clause stood	71
Bethell, Commander, proposes to substitute "delegated" for "granted"	9
Bartlett, Sir Ashmead, replied to by Mr. Gladstone as to concession	13
Boscawen, Mr. G. Amendment to Clause IV. (p. 2, l. 23), after "belief" to insert "or political opinions"	27

[111

THE BILL IN COMMITTEE.—INDEX.

	PAGE
Bryce, Mr., admitted Irish Legislature would differ from Grattan's Parliament	44
Bartley, Mr., on Retention of Irish Members	55
Bolton, Mr. T. H., men on Government Benches prepared to vote for any measure	7
Bitter attack on Government by Mr. Sexton and Mr. Clancy	30
Bolton, Mr. Amendment to Clause IV. (p. 2, line 33), after "taken" to insert "or injuriously affected"	32
O'Brien, Mr., "on prairie value," quoted by Lord Wolmer	34
Bucknill, Mr., quoted Mr. Sexton on Second Reading in debate on Amendment by Mr. Parker Smith...	35
Bolton, Mr., Amendment to Clause XXX., to leave out "shall" and insert "may"	71
Balfour, Mr. G., Amendment to Clause III., "appointment of Judges or Magistrates"	18
Butcher, Mr., Amendment to Clause III.,"criminal conspiracy and combination"	19
Barton, Mr. (for Mr. Carson), Amendment to Clause III., "procedure in criminal matters"	20
Brodrick, Mr., Amendment to Clause III., "the immigration, &c."	21
Bartley, Mr., Amendment to Clause III., "Counties to promote Irish industries"	21
British Majorities against Mr. Gladstone's Scheme	99–104
Boyce, Mr., quotes authorities on Second Chambers, &c., and speaks of Votes being remembered later (Clause I.)	5
Barton, Mr. Dunbar, suggests Mr. Healy take part in Debate on T. W. Russell's Amendment, *in re* "Two Houses" (Clause I.)	4
Bartley, Mr., proposes to insert after "forces," Clause III., "or any police force, &c."	17
Bartley, Mr., Amendment to Clause III., "Bounties"	21
O'Brien, Mr. W., in *Speaker*, quoted by Mr. Balfour in discussion on *Freeman's Journal*	27
Balfour, Mr. A., questions Mr. Gladstone regarding Clause IX.	1
Balfour, Mr. A., replies to Mr. Boyce's threats *in re* Votes on Second Chamber (Clause I.)	5
Balfour, Mr. A., dealing with Mr. Gladstone's opposition to Lord Wolmer's Amendment, quoted the Errington mission as a proceeding without consent, &c., by the House of Commons	16
Balfour, Mr. A., quotes Mr. O'Brien in *Speaker* on clearing out the Castle	27
Balfour, Mr. A., should not leave to Irish Legislature power of Taxing Protestants and Catholics	28
Balfour, Mr. A., comments on Mr. Bolton's Amendment and on Attorney-General	32
Balfour, Mr. A., comments on Lord Wolmer's Amendment to Clause IV.	35
Balfour, Mr. A., asks for information on Education question	41
Balfour, Mr. A., comments on Mr. Bryce's Speech in view of the threatened "Gag"	44
Bartley's, Mr., Amendment on Supremacy	2
Bartley's, Mr., Amendment on Restriction	9
Bartley, Mr., on Motion "That Clause II., &c.," quotes Mr. Dillon, Mr. Davitt, and Mr. Healy with regard to future	13
Blake, Mr., Speech on Mr. Bartley's Amendment, quotes Parnell and Mr. Chamberlain in 1886	3
Brodrick, Mr., Amendment to Clause II. "to restrain powers of Irish Legislature"	10
Bank of Ireland, Discussion on attack made by *Freeman's Journal*	27
Brodrick, Mr., Amendment to Clause V. (p. 3, l. 10) "Prerogatives of Lord Lieutenants"	46
Clause I.	1

THE BILL IN COMMITTEE.—INDEX.

	PAGE
Clause I., Debates on, over 5 Sittings, lasted 29 hours, Mr. Chamberlain moved postponement of (up to IX.)	1
Clause I., Amendment by Mr. Darling	2
Clause I., Amendment by Mr. Bartley	2
Clause I., Amendment by Mr. W. Redmond	3
Clause I., Amendment by Mr. T. W. Russell	4
Clause I., Division on	7
Clause I., as amended in Committee	7
Clause II., over 3 days and occupied 20 hours	7
Clause II., Amendment by Mr. V. Cavendish	8
Clause II., Amendment by Mr. Bartley	9
Clause II., Amendment by Capt. Bethell	9
Clause II., Amendment by Mr. A. Cross	9
Clause II., Amendment by Mr. Brodrick	10
Clause II., Amendment by Sir Henry James	11
Clause II., Amendment by Sir Henry James	11
Clause II., Amendment by Mr. Grant Lawson	12
Clause II., division on	13
Clause II., as amended in Committee	14
Clause III.	14
Clause III., the Debates extended over 11 Sittings and occupied 57 hours	15
Clause III., Amendment by Lord Wolmer	15
Clause III., Amendment by Lord Wolmer	17
Clause III., Amendment by Mr. Bartley	17
Clause III., Amendment by Mr. Byrne	18
Clause III., Amendment by Mr. G. Balfour	18
Clause III., Amendment by Mr. Butcher	19
Clause III., Amendment by Sir Henry James	19
Clause III., Amendments by Mr. Stuart Wortley	20
Clause III., Amendment by Mr. Barton for Mr. Carson	20
Clause III., Amendment by Mr. Brodrick	21
Clause III., Amendment by Mr. Bartley	21
Clause III., Amendment by Mr. Whiteley	22
Clause III., Amendment by Sir J. Lubbock	23
Clause III., Amendment by Sir F. S. Powell	23
Clause III., as amended in Committee	24
Clause IV.	26
Clause IV., the Debate extended over 9 Sittings and lasted 52½ hours	27
Clause IV., Amendment by Mr. G. Boscawen	27
Clause IV., Amendment by Mr. V. Gibbs	28
Clause IV., Amendment by Mr. Mowbray	28
Clause IV., Amendment by Mr. Seton-Karr	29
Clause IV., Amendment by Mr. G. Balfour	30
Clause IV., Amendment by Mr. G. Balfour re-amended	30
Clause IV., Amendment by Mr. Sexton	30

	PAGE
Clause IV., Amendment by Mr. H. Plunkett	31
Clause IV., Amendment by Mr. T. H. Bolton	32
Clause IV., Amendment by Mr. Rentoul	32
Clause IV., Amendment by Lord Wolmer	33
Clause IV., Amendment by Lord Wolmer	34
Clause IV., Amendment to the Amendment of Lord Wolmer, by Mr. Rathbone ...	34
Clause IV., Amendment by Mr. P. Smith	35
Clause IV., Amendment by Mr. D. Plunket	36
Clause IV., Amendment by Mr. D. Plunket	37
Clause IV., Amendment by Mr. Cochrane	38
Clause IV., Amendment by Mr. Cochrane	39
Clause IV., Amendment by Mr. P. Smith	40
Clause IV., as amended in Committee	42
Clause V.	43
Clause V., the debate extended 5 days and occupied 31 hours when the "Gag" was employed	43
Clause V., Amendment by Mr. H. Fisher	43
Clause V., Amendment by Mr. Hanbury	44
Clause V., Amendment by Lord Wolmer	45
Clause V., Amendment by Mr. Brodrick	46
Clause V., Amendment by Marquis of Carmarthen	48
Clause V., Amendment by Lord Wolmer	48
Clause V., several Amendments rejected	48
Clause V., "Gag" applied	48
Clause V., Division on	48
Clause V., as amended in Committee	49
Clauses VI., VII., and VIII., passed without discussion	49
Clauses VI., VII., and VIII., not altered in Committee	50
Clause IX. (Irish Representation in House of Commons)	50
Clause IX., Debate extended over 5 sittings and occupied 261½ hours when "Gag" applied	51
Clause IX., Amendment by Mr. J. Redmond ... ...,	51
Clause IX., Amendment by Mr. Heneage	52
Clause IX., Amendment by Sir J. Lubbock	53
Clause IX., Amendment by Sir C. Dilke	54
Clause IX., Amendment by Mr. Gladstone	55
Clause IX., Division on	56
Clause IX., as amended in Committee	57
Clauses X., XI., XII., XIII., XVII., XX. and XXI. put and negatived without discussion	58
Clauses XIV., XV. and XVI. postponed	58
Clauses XVIII., XIX., XX., XXII., XXIII., XXIV., XXV. and XXVI. put and adopted without discussion	58
Clause XXVII.	59
Clause XXVII., Debate extended over one sitting, lasted 6½ hours	59
Clause XXVII., Amendment by Mr. Sexton	59
Clause XXVII., Amendment by Mr. Morley	60
Clause XXVII., Addition to Mr. Morley's Amendment by Mr. Sexton	61

114]

	PAGE
Clause XXVII., Amendment by Mr. T. W. Russell ...	62
Clause XXVII., amendment by Mr. Seton-Karr ...	62
Clause XXVII., as amended in Committee ...	63
Clause XXVIII., as amended, added to Bill...	64
Clause XXVIII., No. XXV. as amended in Committee	66
Clause XXIX., agreed to	70
Clause XXX. (Police) ...	70
Clause XXX., Debate extended over one sitting, and lasted 5½ hours ...	71
Clause XXX., Amendment by Mr. Bolton ...	71
Clause XXX., Amendment by Mr. Sexton ...	73
Clause XXX., No. XXIX. as amended in Committee	74
Clauses XXXI., XXXII., XXXIII., XXXV., XXXVI. and XXXVIII. added to Bill without discussion ...	75
Clause XXXIX. negatived	75
Clauses XXXIV., XXXVII. and XL. agreed to	75
Clauses, Financial	75
Clauses, Financial, Division on	88
Churchill, Lord Randolph, quoted differences of Church Law as to marriage of First Cousins on Sir J. Lubbock's Amendment to Clause III. re "Marriage" ...	24
Churchill, Lord Randolph, on Mr. Rentoul's Amendment	32
"Censorship of Press," Amendment of Mr. Parker Smith	35
Cochrane, Mr., Amendment to Clause IV. (p. 2, l. 41), to insert "whereby any undue preference, &c." ...	38
Cochrane, Mr. (on behalf of Lord Randolph Churchill), Amendment to Clause IV. (p. 2, l. 4)	39
Carson, Mr., quotes Archbishop Logue in 1873 re Mr. D. Plunket's Amendment	36
Cochrane, Mr., quotes Mr. Bryce on Religious persecution re his Amendment	38
Cross, Mr., "Gas and Water" Amendment, contends nothing should be given Ireland that would not be given Scotland	10
Cross, Mr., characterized by Mr. Gladstone as "ludicrous" ...	10
Clancy, Mr., objects to words being added to Mr. Cochrane's Amendment to Clause IV. ...	39
"Carrying or Using Arms, &c.," Amendment, by Mr. Byrne ...	18
"Clearing out the Castle," Mr. W. O'Brien in, *Speaker*, quoted by Mr. Balfour...	27
Cochrane, Mr., explains design of his Amendment to Clause IV. is to protect Freemasons...	39
Civil Service, Clauses XXVII., XXVIII. and XXIX.	59, 64 and 70
Cranborne, Lord, quotes Mr. Asquith on promised acceptance of supremacy Clause	3
Cavendish, Mr. V., proposes to omit "Restriction" in Clause II.	8
Chairman apologises to Mr. Sexton	18
Carmarthen, Marquis of, Amendment to leave out "or as may be directed by this Act" in Clause V.	48
Chamberlain, Mr., moves to postpone all Clauses up to Clause IX.	1
Chamberlain, Mr., complains of want of information regarding Government intentions	5
Chamberlain, Mr., quotes Mr. Redmond on Supremacy	6
Chamberlain, Mr., quotes Mr. O'Brien on a measure of complete emancipation ...	6
Chamberlain, Mr., quotes Mr. McCarthy on Sir Edward Reed's letter ...	6
Chamberlain, Mr., asks for information of Government intentions	6
Chamberlain, Mr., quotes Mr. John Redmond in August, 1892	12

	PAGE
Chamberlain, Mr., Clause II., asks for specific details as to what Irish Parliament could do...	8
Chamberlain, Mr. : That if Mr. Gladstone meant by Act (matters Irish) it would be playing with the House and the Country	16
Chamberlain, Mr., on Mr. Bartley's Amendment, quoted Mr. Morley in *Nineteenth Century*	22
Cavendish, Mr. Victor, moved to omit the words "with" down to "mentioned," Clause II.	8
Clancy, Mr., in discussion of *Freeman's Journal* attack on Bank of Ireland, contends it was to get Balance Sheets	27
College Green Parliament, the Bank of Ireland, the old Irish House of Commons, Mr. Clancy in discussion on *Freeman's Journal*	27
Clancy, Mr., and Mr. Sexton make bitter attack on Government	30
Clancy, Mr., in debate on Mr. Plunkett's Amendment, says "This was a point, &c." ...	31
Clancy, Mr., moves to add to 4th Sub-section "Whenever the surplus, &c."	95
Chamberlain, Mr., quotes Mr. Dillon on "ruffianly magistrates and policemen" in discussion on *Freeman's Journal*	27
Chamberlain, Mr., asks as to right "to trial by jury"	28
Chamberlain, Mr., in debate on Mr. Plunkett's Amendment, drew attention to its significant phrasing, showing Irish mastery of the Government	31
Chamberlain, Mr., quotes Mr. Dillon, in debate on Lord Wolmer's Amendment	33
Chamberlain, Mr., quoted Lord Spencer on the Land Question, in debate on Mr. Rathbone's Amendment	35
Chamberlain, Mr., called attention that 20 days has elapsed before House informed of subsidising Roman Catholic College	41
Chamberlain, Mr., moves to leave out the words "The Transfer, &c.," and insert "Parliament, &c.," and argued that Bill brought as finality	90
Chamberlain, Mr., comments on Member for North Kerry (Mr. Sexton)	92
Chamberlain, Mr., contends, in final Speech, that Ireland was being asked to pay £1,800,000 less than she ought	96
Chamberlain, Mr., quotes Mr. Dillon ; controversy ensues, when Mr. Dillon proved to be inaccurate	46
Chamberlain, Mr., quotes Mr. Gladstone at Swansea, in 1887, also Lord Rosebery, Sir G. Trevelyan, Mr. Morley, and *United Ireland*	53
Chamberlain, Mr., quotes Mr. Gladstone as to retention of Members	56
Chamberlain, Mr., questions security of British taxpayers if Civil Service salaries on British Exchequer guarantee	60
Chamberlain, Mr., calls attention to numerous facts	75
Chamberlain, Mr., dissented from Mr. Fowler's statement as to difference of £25,000 ...	79
Chaplin, Mr., quotes Mr. Morley on "order in Ireland. and power in the House of Commons"	53
Clark, Dr., in debate on retention, said Government would be defeated if they appealed to the Country	56
Civil Service, Clause XXXVIII., as amended, was added to Bill, also XXIX., with verbal alteration	66
Cohen, Mr., pointed out that not a word of explanation given why cost of collection should be borne by England	81
Clancy, Mr., remarks on Mr. Goschen's observation "able to stand alone"	85
Clancy, Mr., remarks on deficit occurring, the Minister who proposed new tax during next ten or twenty years would be a bold man	89
Collings, Mr., in *re* Mr. Clancy's Amendment, said that Great Britain would be robbed to carry out the scheme of the Government	96

	PAGE
Carson, Mr., observed, according to Clause IX., "Ireland would continue to pay to Imperial Parliament taxes which Mr. Gladstone had described as small and unjust	90
Constabulary, charge for, stated by Mr. Gladstone, in 1886, would not exceed a million ...	82
Constabulary, Mr. Balfour, as he understood Royal Irish Constabulary to be withdrawn on Certificate of New Legislature to Lord-Lieutenant that local police in Counties had been provided	88
Discussion, long, as to what vote on Mr. J. Redmond's Amendment would pledge Committee to... ... ... , ...	88
Debate, in the course of, on Sir Chas. Dilke's Amendment, constant misrepresentations of the Chairman's ruling with regard to Mr. Redmond's motion, &c.	54
Discussion as to precise position of matters re Clause XXX., "Police"... ...	72
Dillon, Mr., in favour of Mr. Sexton's Amendment	73
Discussion with regard to composition and scope of Committee as to General Revenue in future	95
Division on Mr. Morley's Amendment to Clause XXVII.	61
Division on Mr. Sexton's Amendment to Mr. Morley's Amendment	61
Division on Mr. T. W. Russell's Amendment (Mr. Morley undertook to deal with it on report)	62
Division on Mr. Seton-Karr's Amendment, "Superannuation Act, &c."	63
Division on Mr. Bolton's Amendment to Clause XXX. (p. 16, l. 24), to leave out "shall" and insert "may"	72
Division on Mr. Sexton's Amendment to Clause XXX. (p. 16, l. 24), to omit "local" ...	73
Division on Clause XXX., as amended	74
Division on Clauses XXXI., XXXII., XXXIII., XXXVI. and XXXVIII. see Division Lists	103
Division on Clause IX.	56
Division on Mr. Chamberlain's motion to postpone all Clauses up to IX.	1
Division on Mr. Darling's Supremacy Amendment	2
Division on Mr. Bartley's Supremacy Amendment	3
Division on Mr. W. Redmond's Amendment, "Parliament" for "Legislature"... ...	4
Division on Mr. T. W. Russell's Amendment, re Second Chamber	5
Division on Clause I. as part of the Bill	7
Division on Mr. Cavendish's Amendment. re Restriction	8
Division on Commander Bethell's Amendment "Delegated"	9
Division on Mr. Cross's Gas and Water, &c., Amendment	10
Division on Mr. Brodrick's Amendment with regard to Her Majesty diminishing or restraining power of Irish Parliament (Amendment withdrawn)	11
Division on Sir Henry James's Supremacy Amendment (agreed to)	12
Division on Mr. Hanbury's Amendment for Responsible Irish Minister	13
Division on Clause II. as part of the Bill	13
Division on Lord Wolmer's Amendment "to discuss or pass Resolutions." Clause III. ...	16
Division on Lord Wolmer's Amendment "to grant Votes in Supply, &c."	17
Division on Mr. Bartley's Amendment "as to Police Force, &c."	17
Division on Mr. Byrne's Amendment, "arms"	18
Division on Mr. G. Balfour's Amendment	19
Division on Mr. Butcher's Amendment	19

[1.17

	PAGE
Division on Sir Henry James's Amendment	19
Division on Mr. Stuart Wortley's Amendments (defeated)	20
Division on Mr. Barton's (for Mr. Carson) Amendments (defeated)	20
Division on Mr. Brodrick's Amendments (defeated)	21
Division on Mr. Bartley's Amendment, "Bounties to promote Irish Industries,"	22
Division on Mr. Whiteley's Amendment, "Labour"	23
Division on Sir John Lubbock's Amendment. "Banks"	23
Division on Mr. G. Boscawen's Amendment to Clause IV. "or political opinions"	27
Darling, Mr., Amendment to Clause I., quotes Mr. Parnell	2
"Delegated" for "granted" in Clause II., Amendment by Captain Bethell gave rise to three-cornered debate between Mr. Goschen, the Solicitor-General and Mr. Morley	9
Discussion in which grave complaints were made that Unionists were not given fair opportunity	5
"Discuss or pass Resolutions to," Amendment to Clause III., by Lord Wolmer	16
Division on Mr. Vicary Gibbs's Amendment to Clause IV., "New Privilege on Institution belonging to Religious Denomination." (Was withdrawn)	28
Division on Mr. Mowbray's Amendment, "Privilege of Subjects"	29
Division on Mr. Seton-Karr's Amendment, "Without due Process of Law." (Was withdrawn)	29
Division on Mr. Gerald Balfour's Amendment, "Judicial Procedure Unalterable"	30
Division on Mr. Gerald Balfour's Amendment (amended)	30
Division on Mr. Gerald Balfour's Amendment (on Mr. Clancy and Mr. Sexton's attack)	31
Division on Mr. Plunkett's Amendment, "Deprivation of Office"	31
Division on Mr. Bolton's Amendment, "or Injuriously Affected"	32
Division on Mr. Rentoul's Amendment, "Habeas Corpus"	33
Division on Lord Wolmer's Amendment "(b) of an *ex post facto* Character"	34
Division on Lord Wolmer's Amendment, "Impairing the Obligation of Contracts, or"	35
Division on Mr. Rathbone's Amendment to Lord Wolmer's Amendment, "Except with the, &c."	35
Division on Mr. Parker Smith's Amendment "(b) Whereby any Censorship of the Press, &c." (Amendment negatived without division)	35
Division on Mr. David Plunket's Amendment to insert new Sub-section (6)	37
Division on Mr. Plunkett's Amendment after "Legislature" to insert "And after a copy, &c."	38
Division on Mr. Cochrane's Amendment to Clause IV. (p. 2, l. 41), to insert "whereby any undue preference, &c."	39
Division on Mr. Cochrane's Amendment (on behalf of Lord R. Churchill) to Clause IV. (p. 2, l. 4), "whereby any voluntary institution, &c."	40
Division on Mr. Parker Smith's Amendment (p. 2, l. 41), to Clause IV., insert as a new Section "(7) whereby the actions, &c."	41
Division on Mr. Hayes Fisher's Amendment to Clause V. (p. 3, l. 6), after "Lieutenant" to insert "or other chief executive, &c." Government accepted the addition	43
"Due Process of Law," Mr. Seton-Karr's Amendment	29
Discussion on proper interpretation of words "Due Process of Law"	29
Discussion as to protection of minorities, &c., following Mr. Rentoul's Amendment	33
Davitt, Mr., on "Prairie Value," quoted by Lord Wolmer	34
Debate on Mr. Rathbone's Amendment continued amidst much interruption from the Irish Benches	35

THE BILL IN COMMITTEE.—INDEX.

	PAGE
Discussion on action of Government *re* Mr. Plunkett's Amendment	31
Droit Administratif, Mr. P. Smith's Amendment to prevent	40
Discussion, heated, on Amendment by Mr. Arnold Forster	48
"Did not disguise the difficulties of the position" in Speech of Solicitor-General on Lord Wolmer's Amendment	16
Discussion on attack made by *Freeman's Journal* on Bank of Ireland	27
Dillon, Mr., quoted by Mr. Chamberlain, "ruffianly magistrates and policemen"	27
Dillon Mr., quoted by Mr. Chamberlain, "when they came out of the struggle"	33
Dilke, Sir Charles, Amendment to Clause IX. (p. 4, l. 27), after "constituencies" to insert the word "hereinafter"	54
Discussion takes place regarding worth of the Veto	48
Division on Clauses VI., VII. and VIII. (passed without discussion)	49
Division on Mr. J. Redmond's Amendment to Clause IX.	52
Division on Mr. Heneage's Amendment to leave out from "day" to end of Sub-section 2 to Clause IX.	53
Division on Sir J. Lubbock's Amendment after "day" to insert "existing constituencies, etc.," (negatived) Clause IX.	53
Division on Sir Charles Dilke's Amendment after "constituencies" to insert the word "hereinafter," Clause IX.	55
Division on Mr. Gladstone's Amendment to omit Sections 3 and 4 to Clause IX.	56
Division on Clause IX.	56
Division on Mr. Sexton's Amendment to Clause XXVII. (withdrawn by leave)	60
Division on Mr. Hanbury's Amendment to Clause V. (line 6), after words "Lord Lieutenant" to leave out words "on behalf of Her Majesty," and insert "with the approval of Her Majesty, &c."	44
Division on Lord Wolmer's Amendments, Clause V. (p. 3. l. 10), after Sub-section 1 to insert "(1.) For the due, &c."	46
Division on Mr. Brodrick's Amendment to Clause V. (p. 3, l. 10), after Sub-section 1, to insert "the Lord Lieutenant, &c."	48
Division on Marquis of Carmarthen's Amendment to Clause V., to leave out words "or as may be directed by this Act" (eventually withdrawn)	48
Division on Clause V.	48
Divisions on Bill	99 to 104

Executive powers. Mr. Gladstone states Bill does not create	10
"*Ex post facto* character." Amendment by Lord Wolmer	33
"Except with the consent &c.," Amendment by Mr. Rathbone to Amendment of Lord Wolmer	34
Establishment of Roman Catholic University would be dealt with and answered when whole Clause (IV.) before House (*re* Mr. D. Plunket's Amendment)	36
Education Question : Information asked by Mr. Balfour	41
Enemies of Ireland ; language of *Irish Independent* referred to by Mr. Wm. Kenny	27

Fowler, Mr., deals with points raised in debate on Clause II., regarding veto and supremacy	13
Factories, Workshops, &c., Amendment by Mr. Whiteley to Clause III.	22
Freeman's Journal, attack by, on Bank of Ireland. Discussion; procedure adopted by *Freeman's Journal* in regard to "black list"	27

THE BILL IN COMMITTEE.—INDEX.

	PAGE
Fisher, Mr. Hayes, Amendment to Clause V. (p. 3, l. 6), after "Lieutenant" to insert "or other chief executive, &c."	43
Forster, Mr. Arnold. Amendment dealing with prerogative of mercy	48
Fowler, Mr., in reply to Mr. Goschen, puts error in calculation down at £350,000, and speaks generally on the Finances of Ireland. Took Constabulary at full charge	79
Fowler, Mr., replies to Mr. Brodrick	80
Fallaciousness of Fly-Sheet distributed by the Hon. Member for Surrey shown by Sir Wm. Harcourt; replying to Mr. Brodrick could not see how the Prime Minister arrived at the results stated in Speech of 1886, could not help it if hon. gentleman chose to rely on figures of that description, also said Government had had to offer Irish bribes as the price of peace	82

Goschen, Mr., How was Lord Lieutenant's Cheque to be honoured	60
Goschen, Mr., replies to Mr. Gladstone as to Civil Service	65-69
Goschen, Mr., speaks on the question of the cost of Collection of Revenue and further as to the Grant of £500,000, and that Ireland could not do without this contribution, and generally on finance as set forth in Bill; also replies to Mr. Gladstone as to Spirit Duties, 1853	84-85
Goschen, Mr., solicits Statement from Mr. Fowler	93
Goschen, Mr., speaks on use of word "Delegated" in three-cornered debate with the Solicitor-General and Mr. Morley	9
Goschen, Mr., moved to report progress, discussion in which grave complaints were made as to fair play to Unionists	14
Goschen, Mr., on Sir J. Lubbock's Amendment to Clause III., pointed out arrangement would give different laws of exchange	23
Goschen, Mr., describes Mr. Morley's reply as a revelation of chaos	47
Goschen, Mr., observes Lord Lieutenant was to have three capacities	47
Goschen, Mr., on all fours with present arrangement, save Chief Secretary, would be replaced by the Lord Lieutenant	47
Gladstone, Mr., replies to Mr. Chamberlain re Clause IX.	1
Gladstone, Mr., apologises for Mr. Parnell's "dangerous claims," and that Mr. Parnell had accepted Bill 1886 Amendment would weaken supremacy and would be a bar sinister	2
Gladstone, Mr., opposes Mr. W. Redmond's Amendment re Legislature	3
Gladstone, Mr., advocates second chamber as check and restraint	6
Gladstone, Mr., admits adjustment of details in retention insurmountable, and speaks of waiting for formation of public opinion	6
Gladstone, Mr., asks Mr. Chamberlain if he will accept Bill if Amendment accepted	8
Gladstone, Mr., explains regarding marriage laws, &c.	8
Gladstone, Mr., supports restrictions by reference to U.S. Constitution	9
Gladstone, Mr., characterises Mr. Cross's Gas and Water Amendment as ludicrous	10
Gladstone, Mr., to Mr. Balfour, states, as to Mr. Brodrick's Amendment, Bill does not create executive powers	10
Gladstone, Mr., on perfect and bonâ fide equality between two Houses	11
Gladstone, Mr., accepts Sir H. James's Amendment on Supremacy	12
Gladstone, Mr., to Sir Ashmead-Bartlett, states he made concession, re Supremacy, on Second Reading	13
Gladstone, Mr., replying to Lord Wolmer's Amendment (p. 1, l. 19) said it would be unwise to make declaration of power without means to support it	15
Gladstone, Mr., in reply to Mr. Balfour, referred that gentleman to Clause IX.	16

	PAGE
Gladstone, Mr., in Debate on Mr Bartley's Amendment, "Or any Police Force, &c.," said Irish Legislature ought to be in position to re-create the Irish Constabulary ...	17
Gladstone, Mr., apologises to Mr. Sexton	18
Gladstone, Mr., accepts Mr. Sexton's contention as to crippling Irish Legislature... ...	18
Gorst, Sir John, quotes phrase subordinate Parliament from Statute of 1791	6
Gorst, Sir John, quotes Act of 1791 and Act of 1783 in Debate on Motion "That Clause I., &c."	6
Gorst, Sir John, refers to difficulty arising in sending Irish representatives to Labour Conferences	22
"Gag" Resolutions discussed	44
"Gag," Mr. Balfour deals with matters settled by	91
"Gag" applied 56, 74,	97
Gladstone, Mr., gave opinion of Irish Parliament dealing with Premiums	22
Gladstone, Mr., admits on Sir J. Lubbock's Amendment to Clause III. that Ireland would be treated as foreign country in case of Bills	23
Gladstone, Mr., opposes Amendment of Sir F. S. Powell to Clause III., "Marriage and Divorce"	23
Gladstone, Mr., on Mr. Rentoul's Amendment	32
Gladstone, Mr., on Lord Wolmer's Amendment to Clause IV.	34
Gladstone, Mr., moves the omission of Sections 3 and 4 to Clause IX.	55
Gladstone, Mr., contends safeguards sufficient, re Mr. David Plunket's Amendment ...	36
Gladstone, Mr., objected to Mr. Cochrane's Amendment	40
Gladstone, Mr., foundation of a Roman Catholic College possible	41
Gladstone, Mr., replying, denies deprivation of essential powers	52
Gladstone, Mr., Land Question was not reserved for six years	52
Gladstone, Mr., opposes Amendment of Sir Chas. Dilke, and described scheme as being "in the rough, &c."	54
Gladstone, Mr., stated his determination to defeat Mr. Chamberlain's intentions ...	56
Gladstone, Mr., deals with possibilities of change, &c.	65
Gladstone, Mr., contends Bill follows English principle as to Civil Service servants ...	65
Gladstone, Mr., further replies to Mr. Goschen re Retirement of Civil Service officers ...	65
Gladstone, Mr., Government do not impose upon Lord Lieutenant the necessity for reduction	72
Gladstone, Mr., opposes Mr. Sexton's Amendment to Clause XXX. to omit "local" ...	73
Gladstone, Mr., could not assent to Amendment of Mr. J. Redmond to omit first Sub-section	52
Gladstone, Mr., on question raised by Mr. A. Balfour as to Collection of Revenues ...	89
Gladstone, Mr., correcting Mr. Chamberlain, "a continuing settlement"	88
Gladstone, Mr., grants the Land Question as an obligation of honor in reply to Mr. Chamberlain, also speaks of Clauses already settled	91
Gladstone, Mr., replying to Mr. Balfour, explained words referred to, introduced to show Clause IX. was no part of honorable compact between Great Britain and Ireland ...	92
Gibbs, Mr. Vicary, Amendment to Clause IV., "Institutions belonging to Religious Denominations"	28
Gladstone, Mr., explains as to surplus of £500,000 in re Mr. Clancy's Amendment ...	96
Gladstone, Mr., replying to Mr. J. Redmond, said his objection remained in full... ...	96
Healy, Mr., "I am not such a fool," in reply to Mr. Barton's invitation to take part in debate on Mr. T. W. Russell's Amendment (Clause I.) "Two Houses"	4

[121]

	PAGE
Habeas Corpus, suspension of, Attorney-General in reply to Lord Wolmer	28
Habeas Corpus, suspension of, argued against in debate on Mr. Rentoul's Amendment	32
Haldane, Mr., on Lord Wolmer's Amendment to Clause IV.	34
Heneage, Mr., Amendment to Clause V. (p. 4, l. 27), to leave out from "day" to end of Sub-section (11), quotes Mr. Gladstone in 1886	2
Hanbury, Mr., Amendment to Clause V., "approval of H.M. by Secretary of State"	44
Harrington, Mr., speaks with reference to Chamberlain-Duignan correspondence...	46
Hobhouse, Mr., quotes John Redmond on "the Formal compact" in re Bartley's Amendment to Clause I.	3
Harcourt, Sir William, refers to "the fallacy that runs through the whole of the fly-sheet which has been distributed by the hon. member for Surrey"	82
Harcourt, Sir William, to Mr. Jackson, denies words attributed to him	83
James, Sir H., Amendment re Equal Powers of Two Houses	11
James, Sir H., Amendment, re Supremacy, on Clause II.	10
James, Sir H., Amendment as to "Supreme Power and Authority of Parliament," Clause II.	10
"Injuriously affected," Amendment by Mr. Bolton to Clause IV.	32
James, Sir H., on Mr. Rentoul's Amendment	32
James, Sir H., on Lord Wolmer's Amendment to Clause IV.	33
Imperial Supremacy : Mr. Darling's Amendment	2
Imperial Supremacy : Mr. Bartley's Amendment	3
Imperial Supremacy, that the concession regarding, was made on 2nd Reading, statement made by Mr. Gladstone in reply to Sir Ashmead-Bartlett	13
Irish Legislature ought to be in a position to re-create the Irish Constabulary in speech by Mr. Gladstone in Debate on Mr. Bartley's Amendment	17
Irish Independent, of 31st March, 1893, as to enemies of Ireland, referred to by Mr. Kenny	27
Jones, Mr. Atherly, refers to Mr. Boyce's threat re Vote on Second Chamber (Clause I.)	5
Irish Legislature, withdrawal of power of, as to University Education in Ireland ; question by Mr. Sexton on	28
Irish Government, powers of, Attorney-General explains, in debate on Mr. Seton-Karr's Amendment	29
Interpretation of words "due process of law" discussion	29
Irish mastery of the Government—attention drawn by Mr. Chamberlain, in debate on Mr. Plunkett's Amendment	31
Irish Government allowed to mark down opponents and imprison without trial, asserted in discussion on Mr. Rentoul's Amendment	33
"Impossible to pass Legislation without making promises ;" Mr. Rathbone in moving his Amendment to Amendment of Lord Wolmer	34
"Interruption of meeting for legal purposes ;" Amendment by Mr. Parker Smith	35
Index	105
Jackson, Mr., did not consider Chancellor of Exchequer did himself justice, and that he had hardly behaved fairly with members of Opposition	82

	PAGE
Karr, Mr. Seton-, Amendment (Clause IV., p. 2, l. 31), to leave out "without due process of law" ...	29
Karr, Mr. Seton-, Amendment to Clause XXVII., "The Superannuation Act, &c." ...	62
Karr, Mr. Seton-, objects to Mr. Storey's "Sordid Policy" observation...	60
Karr, Mr. Seton-, charges Government with breach of faith with the Committee *re* Mr. Morley's Amendment ...	61
Kenny, Mr. Wm., contends that attack on Bank of Ireland by *Freeman's Journal* caused by Unionist Directors ; also quotes Journal as to "black list" and language of the *Irish Independent* ...	27
Kenny, Mr. Wm., points out that in Bill of 1886 Government did what they now objected to, *re* Mr. D. Plunket's Amendment ...	36
Kenny, Mr. Wm., expresses his objections to Mr. Morley's Amendment to Clause XXVII.	61
Lubbock, Sir John, Amendment to Clause III., "Banks" ...	23
Lubbock, Sir John, Amendment to Clause IX. (p. 4, l. 27), after "day" to insert "Existing Constituencies, &c.," in support, pointed out under Bill Ireland would bear one-fortieth of the burden, &c. ...	54
Lubbock, Sir John, points out that Ireland's Parliamentary representation was more than 15 per cent., her contribution to expenditure was under 8 per cent., &c. ...	80
Lubbock, Sir John, moves to omit Sub-sections 2, 3, 4 and 5 ...	93
Lubbock, Sir John, argues in favour of Amendment ...	54
Labouchere, Mr., on Second House, in Mr. Russell's Amendment (Clause I.) ...	4
Labouchere, Mr., thinks total exclusion best plan ...	56
Labouchere, Mr. (later on), would not vote according to his conviction ...	56
"Ludicrous," Mr. A. Cross's Amendment to Clause II., so characterised by Mr. Gladstone	9
Language of *Irish Independent* referred to by Mr. W. Kenny "with regard to the enemies of Ireland" ...	27
"Law," after (Clause IV.), Amendment to insert "in accordance, &c." ...	30
Lawson, Mr. Grant, Amendment "no laws repugnant, &c." ...	13
"Language in debate one thing, in Clause another"—significant remark by Mr. Sexton on his Amendment to Clause IV. ...	30
Mowbray, Mr., Amendment to Clause IV. (p. 2. l. 30), after "whereby" to insert "the privileges or, &c." ...	28
McCarthy, Mr. Justin, accepts Second Chamber in deference to Irish Unionist fears, &c. (Clause I.) ...	5
McCarthy, Mr. Justin, on Sir Edward Reed's Letter...	6
Motion to omit words "With" down to "mentioned" in Clause II., by Mr. Victor Cavendish ...	8
Motion to insert words "To discuss or pass resolutions or to" after "power to" (p. 1, l. 19), by Lord Wolmer ...	15
Motion "That Clause II., as amended, stand part of the Bill" ...	13
"Marriage and Divorce." Amendment of Sir F. S. Powell to Clause III. ...	23
Matthews, Mr. H., states under Bill Government could make quite different Code of Criminal Law ...	8
Marriage Laws, Mr. Gladstone explains regarding ...	8
Minister in both Houses of Parliament responsible for Irish Affairs ...	12
Murray, Mr. G., argued there was nothing in the Bill to prevent Octroi Duties ...	13
Mundella, Mr., advocated freedom in matter, in speaking on Mr. Whiteley's Amendment *re* "Factories, &c." ...	22

	PAGE
Morley, Mr., on "Delegated" and "Granted" ...	9
Morley, Mr., Proposed New Sub-section to Clause XXVII. ...	60
Morley, Mr., suggested words to add to Mr. Cochrane's Amendment to Clause IV. ...	39
Morley, Mr., refuses to accept Mr. P. Smith's Amendment to Clause IV., as Irish Government not likely to adopt *droit administratif* ...	40
Morley, Mr., replies to various Questions ...	59
Morley, Mr., explains Home Secretary would draw up instructions ...	47
Morley, Mr., that Home Secretary would be called to account for action of Lord Lieutenant	47
Minority on discussion of Mr. W. Redmond's motion to substitute "Parliament" for "Legislature" (negatived) 40, made up of certain Radical and Irish Members ...	3
Minorities in Ireland, pledges of Government Candidates to protect ...	33
Morley, Mr., says Clause XXVII. was simply to protect vested interests ...	60
Morley, Mr., replies to Mr. Chamberlain, *re* Clause XXVII. ..	60
Morley, Mr., accepts Mr. Sexton's Amendment to his Amendment ...	61
Morley, Mr., undertakes to deal with Mr. T. W. Russell's Amendment on report ...	62
Morley, Mr., explains scheme and scope of Clauses at length in debate on Clause XXVIII.	65
Morley, Mr., in reply to Mr. Matthews, explains *re* withdrawals ...	72
Matthews, Mr., quotes Chief Secretary ...	72
Matthews, Mr.: And further, in reply to Mr. Morley, also points out "shall" (Mr. Bolton's Amendment) becomes inappropriate ...	72
Matthews, Mr.: And points out to Mr. Gladstone obligation on officers by "shall" reduce	72
Nolan, Captain, contends that dividing the amount of population Ireland paid 10s. per head instead of 3s. 6d. as stated by Mr. Brodrick ...	94

"On Prairie Value," quoted from Mr. O'Brien by Lord Wolmer ...	34
O'Brien, Mr. W., on a measure of complete Emancipation ...	6
On the Motion "That Clause II., as amended, stand part of the Bill" ...	13
Octroi duties, Mr. G. Murray argued there was nothing in the Bill to prevent ...	13
"Or to entertain or grant Votes in Supply, &c.," Amendment by Lord Wolmer ...	17
"Or any Police Force, &c.," Amendment by Mr. Bartley to Clause III.	17
"Or injuriously affected," Amendment by Mr. Bolton to Clause IV. ...	32
"Of an *ex post facto* character," Amendment by Lord Wolmer to Clause IV. (p. 2, l. 33) ...	34

Precedent undesirable and unfair. Debate on Mr. D. Plunket's Amendment to Clause IV.	37
Postponement of all Clauses up to Clause IX., moved by Mr. Chamberlain ...	1
Parnell, Mr., Mr. Gladstone refers to dangerous claims of	2
Parnell, Mr., quoted by Mr. Blake ...	3
"Parliament could not divest itself of its powers," contended by Sir John Rigby in debate on Motion " that Clause I., &c." ...	6
"Peace, Order, and Good Government of Ireland," Irish Legislature responsible for ...	18
"Protectionist proclivities on part of Irish People," quoted by Mr. Chamberlain from paper by Mr. Morley in *Nineteenth Century* ...	22
Prerogative of Mercy, Amendment by Mr. Arnold Forster ...	48
Powell, Sir F. S., Amendment to Clause III. "(2.) Marriage and Divorce" ...	23
"Political Opinions," Amendment of Mr. G. Boscawen to Clause IV. ...	27
"Power of suspending Habeas Corpus," Attorney-General in reply to Lord Wolmer ...	28

THE BILL IN COMMITTEE.—INDEX. 121

	PAGE
Powers of Irish Government explained by Attorney-General *re* Mr. Seton-Karr's Amendment	29
Plunkett, Mr. H., Amendment to Clause IV. (p. 2, l. 1) after word "Law" to insert "or any person, &c."	31
Plunket, Mr. David, Amendment to Clause IV. (p. 33, l. 2) after "or" to insert "(6) Affecting the Constitution, &c."	36
Pledges of Government, Candidates at Election to protect Minorities in Ireland	33
Provision existed in the American Constitution such as he had put in his Amendment (Lord Wolmer)	34
"Promises which could not be carried out," Mr. Rathbone in moving his Amendment to Amendment of Lord Wolmer	34
Plunket, Mr. David, Amendment to Clause IV. (p. 2, l. 39), after "Legislature" to insert "And after a copy, &c."	37
Plunket, Mr. David, quotes Prime Minister, shewing they were to have a 3-fold protection against unfair treatment	37
Plunket, Mr. D., instances fall of Government 20 years ago. Demands of Irish Roman Catholic prelates as to Dublin University irreconcilable ; also quoted Dr. Walsh on subject in 1886, &c., in support of his Amendment to Clause IV.	36
Plunkett, Mr., drew attention to the change from Bill of 1886	48
Plunket, Mr. D., University Representation	55

Royal Irish Constabulary to be withdrawn so soon as new Irish Legislature certified to Lord Lieutenant Local Police had been provided	72
Retention of Members, Mr. Atherley Jones on	56
Retention of Members, Sir Henry James on	56
Retention of Members, Sir William Harcourt on	56
Retention of Members, Mr. Darling on	56
Retention of Members, Mr. Balfour on	91
Retention of Members, Mr. Chamberlain on	56
Retention of Members, Mr. Rathbone on	55
Retention of Members, Mr. Gladstone on	56
Retention of Members, Mr. Wallace on	41
Retention of Members, Sir Edward Reed on	6
Retention of Members, Mr. Labouchere on	56
Retention of Members, Mr. Bartley on	55
Retention of Members, Mr. David Plunket on	55
Retention of Members, Mr. J. Redmond on	51
Retention of Members, Dr. Clark on	56
Rathbone, Mr., Amendment to the Amendment of Lord Wolmer to add, "Except with the consent, &c."	34
Russell, Mr. T. W., Amendment *re* "Two Houses"	4
Russell, Mr. T. W., quotes Mr. Redmond on Parliamentary Compact"	12
Russell, Mr., said the Irish people looked on Home Rule as a way to cheapen land and subsidise manufacture	22
Redmond, Mr., on "Formal Compact," quoted by Mr. Hobhouse	3
Redmond, Mr., on "Supremacy"	6
Redmond, Mr., on "Parliamentary Compact"	12

[125

	PAGE
Redmond, Mr. W., Motion to substitute "Parliament" for "Legislature" in Clause I., opposed by Mr. Gladstone on ground that Colonial Assemblies described as "Legislatures"	3
"Restraining powers of Irish Legislature," Amendment to Clause II., by Mr. Brodrick ...	10
"Reducing the House of Commons to a state of impotence" in speech by Mr. Sexton on Amendment of Mr. P. Smith	35
Rigby, Sir John, states Parliament cannot divest itself of its powers (in Debate on retention of Clause I.)	6
Responsible Minister for Irish affairs, Amendment by Mr. Hanbury to Clause II. ...	12
"Ruffianly Magistrates and Policemen," quotation of Mr. Dillon by Mr. Chamberlain ...	27
Rentoul, Mr., Amendment to Clause IV. (p. 2, l. 33) "Suspending or prejudicially, &c." ...	32
Redmond, Mr. J., Amendment to Clause IX. to leave out Sub-section 1.	51
Redmond, Mr. J., present scheme of Re-distribution imperfect	54
Reed, Sir E.: Mr. McCarthy in letter says, supremacy must be preserved by a clear and distinct clause	6
Reed, Sir E., on wrongful acts being wrongful acts still	6
Reed, Sir E.: Retention of Irish Members for all purposes would be playing false to country	6
Reed, Sir E., states Bill was being discussed under "dangerous conditions"	10
Restrictions supported by Mr. Gladstone by reference to U.S. Constitution	9
Russell, Mr. T. W., Amendment to Clause XXVII., to add end of Sub-section, "and Sub-section 2, &c."	62
Russell, Mr., gave some examples of injustice of method employed, re Sir Chas. Dilke's Amendment	54
Russell, Mr., strongly objects to provisions of Clause XXVIII., and cites instances of injustice likely to occur	66
Russell, Mr., considered Mr. Sexton had shown his hand as to treatment Ulster would receive	73
Redmond, Mr. J., explains as to surplus, re Mr. Clancy's Amendment	96
Rathbone, Mr., protests against omission of Sections 3 and 4 of Clause IX.	55
Redmond, Mr. J., in favour of Mr. Sexton's Amendment to Clause XXX.	73
Redmond, Mr. J., advocates appointment of Special Commission on Taxes and Revenues of Ireland	80
Redmond, Mr. J., Moves omission of the first Sub-section in order to raise clear issue ...	88
Rentoul, Mr., spoke with reference to the relative cost of the police in England, Scotland, and Ireland, referred to by the Chancellor of the Exchequer	84
Safeguards, sufficient contention of, Mr. Gladstone re Mr. D. Plunket's Amendment ...	36
Supremacy, Mr. Redmond on, quoted by Mr. Chamberlain in speech on Motion "that Clause I. stand part of the Bill"	6
Sir Edward Reed's letter, Mr. McCarthy on, quoted by Mr. Chamberlain in speech on Motion "that Clause I., &c."	6
"Supremacy must be preserved by means of a clear and distinct clause" asserted by Sir Edward Reed in debate on Motion "that Clause I., &c."	6
Supremacy, a series of Amendments dealing with, defeated	17
Saunders, Mr., speaks on Mr. Russell's Second Chamber Amendment (Clause I.) ...	5
Solicitor-General "did not disguise the difficulties of the position, &c."	16
Suspension of Habeas Corpus, Attorney-General in reply to Lord Wolmer	28
Sub-section 5, quoted by Attorney-General in reply to Mr. Chamberlain	29

	PAGE
Solicitor-General, opinion quoted by Mr. G. Balfour *re* his Amendment to Clause IV.	30
Significant remark by Mr. Sexton on his Amendment to Clause IV.	30
Storey, Mr. S., votes for Cavendish Amendment, because of promise to constituents to vote for Bills with matter delegated specifically set out	8
Sexton, Mr., against by Byrne's Amendment, and complains of Chairman	18
Sexton, Mr., asks if it is proposed to withdraw power from Irish Legislature as to University Education in Ireland	28
Sexton, Mr., Amendment (to Mr. G. Balfour's Amendment) to Clause IV., "regard being had to" for "in accordance"	30
Sexton, Mr., and Mr. Clancy make bitter attack on Government	30
Significant phrasing of Mr. Plunkett's Amendment to Clause IV., attention drawn by Mr. Chamberlain	31
Suspension of Habeas Corpus argued against in course of debate on Mr. Rentoul's Amendment	32
Smith, Mr. Parker, Amendment to Clause IV. (l. 2, p. 33) after word "or" to insert "(6) whereby any, &c."	35
Sexton, Mr., makes violent speech against Mr. Parker Smith's Amendment	35
Storey, Mr., speaks of "sordid policy," in *re* Clause XXVII.	60
Smith, Mr. Parker, Amendment to Clause IV. (p. 2, l. 41), to insert "(7) Whereby the, &c."	35
Sexton, Mr., Amendment to Clause XXVII. (p. 15, l. 21), to omit "and Land Commissioners of Ireland." (Amendment withdrawn)	59
Sexton, Mr., proposed to insert at beginning of the Amendment (Mr. Morley's), "Sub-section 1 of," Clause XXVII.	61
Sexton, Mr., moved to omit "local" (p. 16, l. 24), Clause XXX.	73
Sexton, Mr., replies to Mr. D. Plunket on his speaking in support of Amendment	36
Smith, Mr. Parker, points out design of his Amendment is to prevent Irish Government from adopting *droit administratif*	40
Sexton, Mr., replies to Mr. Chamberlain *re* Clause 27	60
Sexton, Mr., argues in support of his Amendment that there would be no suitable local authority under which to place police	73
Sexton, Mr., could only countenance the withholding of the power of collecting the taxes from the Irish Legislature as a provisional arrangement	73
Saunderson, Colonel, quotes Mr. Dillon's cross-examination at Cork in 1891	73
Saunderson, Colonel, speaks as to a later Amendment providing for payment of tribute	8
"Two houses, and of] the Legislative Council and" Amendment (Clause I.) by Mr. T. W. Russell, advocated by Mr. Labouchere, Mr. Justin McCarthy, Mr. Gladstone, Mr. Boyce, &c.	4
Three-cornered debate takes place between Mr. Goschen, the Solicitor-General and Mr. Morley, on Captain Bethell's Amendment to substitute "delegated" for "granted" in Clause II.	9
Temple, Sir Richard, argued Ireland differed from smaller European powers being defended	94
Unionist Party and Government again voted together, and Irish party joined by portion of Radical section	31
Ulster, fears respecting—comment by Attorney-General on Mr. Rentoul's Amendment	32
Unionist character of Directors of *Freeman's Journal* cause of attack by paper on Bank of Ireland ; Mr. W. Kenny in discussion	27
University Education in Ireland, question asked by Mr. Sexton in discussion on Mr. V. Gibbs's Amendment	28

[127

	PAGE
Violent speech against the Amendment of Mr. Parker Smith by Mr. Sexton. ...	35
Wallace, Dr., speaks on Mr. Russell's Amendment *re* Second Chamber (Clause I) ...	5
"When they came out of the struggle," quoted by Mr. Chamberlain from Mr. Dillon ...	33
"Whereby any Censorship of the Press, &c." Amendment by Mr. Parker Smith... ...	35
Wallace, Mr. R., on Retention of Members	41
Wallace, Mr., Humorous Speech	55
Wolmer, Lord, Moved to insert in Clause III. (p. 1, l. 19) after "to" to insert "discuss, or pass resolutions, or to"	16
Wolmer, Lord, Moved to insert after "laws," "or to entertain or grant votes in supply, &c."	17
Wolmer, Lord, Moved to insert (p. 2, l. 33, Clause IV.) "(6) of an *ex post facto* character"	34
Wolmer, Lord, Moved to insert (p. 2, l. 33) "impairing the obligation of Contracts or " ...	35
Wolmer, Lord, Moved to insert (p. 3, l. 10) after Sub-section 1 "(1) for the due enforcement, &c."	46
Wolmer, Lord, Amendment to Clause V., to leave out "on the advice of the said Executive Committee"	48
Whiteley, Mr., Amendment to Clause III., "Factories, Workshops, &c."	22
Wyndham, Mr., quotes Mr. Fowler, also Mr. Gladstone and Mr. Morley	73

www.ingramcontent.com/pod-product-compliance
Lightning Source LLC
Chambersburg PA
CBHW022138160426
43197CB00009B/1338